10

MINUTE GUIDE TO

PAYING FOR GRAD SCHOOL

by Ellen Lichtenstein

alpha
books

A Division of Macmillan Publishing
A Simon & Schuster Macmillan Company
1633 Broadway, New York, NY 10019-6785

International Standard Book Number:0-02-861165-9
Library of Congress Catalog Card Number: 96-085371

98 97 96   8 7 6 5 4 3 2 1

Interpretation of the printing code: the rightmost double-digit number is the year of the book's first printing; the rightmost single-digit number is the number of the book's printing. For example, a printing code of 96-1 shows that this copy of the book was printed during the first printing of the book in 1996.

Printed in the United States of America

Publisher: Theresa Murtha
Development Editor: Jennifer Perillo
Production Editor: Mike Thomas
Copy Editor: Theresa Mathias
Cover Designer: Dan Armstrong
Designer: Kim Scott
Indexer: Debra Myers
Production Team: Angela Calvert, Christine Tyner, Karen Walsh

CONTENTS

INTRODUCTION   VI

1 GOING TO GRADUATE SCHOOL   1

Benefits of Getting Your Graduate Degree 1
Education and Earnings 1
Exploring Your Options 2
Working versus Going to Graduate School 3
Seeking Practical Advice 6
Summary 6

2 UNDERSTANDING YOUR OPTIONS   7

Deciding Between Full- or Part-Time Study 7
Understanding Your Choices 9
Choosing the Right School 10
Academic Quality of the School and Program 10
College Costs 12
Other Factors to Consider 13
Summary 15

3 ESTIMATING THE COSTS   16

Financial Planning 16
Assessing Tuition 17
Estimating Personal Expenses 19
Totaling the Costs 21
Summary 22

4 UNDERSTANDING FINANCIAL AID   23

Sources of Financial Aid 23
Classification of Financial Aid 23
Forms of Financial Aid 26
How Many Students Receive Financial Aid? 27
Summary 30

5 UNDERSTANDING FEDERAL LOANS   31

Borrowing from Your Uncle 31
Perkins Loans 32
Stafford Loan Program 33
Subsidized Stafford Loans 35
Unsubsidized Stafford Loans 36
Summary 38

6 SEEKING PRIVATE LOANS AND ALTERNATIVE FUNDING   39

Going the Private Funding Route 39
Funding Through Your Job 42
Summary 44

7 DISCOVERING FINANCIAL AID FROM STATE SOURCES   45

Exploring All Options 45
State Loans 46
Matching Student Grants 46
Summary 47

**8 FEDERAL WORK-STUDY (FWS) AND OTHER WORK
    PROGRAMS   48**
Federal Work-Study (FWS) 48
Assistantships 50
Service-Related Grants and Fellowships 51
Cooperative Education 52
Internships 52
Summary 53

**9 SEEKING OUT PRIVATE GRANTS, FELLOWSHIPS,
    AND SCHOLARSHIPS   54**
Understanding the Types and Sources of Outright
    Awards 54
Exploring Available Funding Sources 55
How Awards Affect Financial Aid Eligibility 61
Summary 61

10 RESEARCHING FEDERAL GRANTS   62
Doing Your Homework 62
Researching All Sources 63
Summary 67

11 PREPARING GRANT APPLICATIONS   68
Application Procedures 68
Application Strategies 70
Writing Style and Organization 71
Basic Proposal Structure 71
For Further Information... 72
Summary 73

12 RESEARCHING SPECIAL FUNDING OPPORTUNITIES   74
Special Funding Opportunities 74
Researching the Opportunities 74
Opportunities for Women and Minorities 75
Opportunities for Veterans 78
Opportunities for Students Studying Overseas 78
Opportunities for Disabled Students 79
Opportunities for Foreign Students 79
Summary 80

13 ESTIMATING YOUR FINANCIAL STANDING   81
Calculating Your Net Worth 81
Getting Your Figures on Paper 83
Estimating How Much More Money You Need 85
Summary 85

14 PREPARING A SAVINGS PLAN   86
Saving for Your Graduate Education 86
Saving Short Term 87
Researching Your Savings and Investment Options 88
Special College Savings Plans 89
Summary 90

15   BEGINNING THE FINANCIAL AID APPLICATION PROCESS   91

Overview of the Application Process 91
Taking the First Step 91
Finding Other Sources of Aid 93
Getting the Right Applications 93
Managing the Application Process 94
Summary 96

16   FILING AND PROCESSING APPLICATION FORMS   97

The FAFSA 97
The Student Aid Report (SAR) 100
Special Circumstances 103
Financial Aid PROFILE 104
Summary 104

17   MANAGING DEADLINES   105

Beating Deadlines 105
Preparing a Deadline Calendar 106
Testing Deadlines 107
Admission Deadlines 108
Financial Aid Deadlines 108
Summary 110

18   UNDERSTANDING THE FINANCIAL AWARD PACKAGE   111

Getting the Package 111
Understanding the Award Letter 112
Choosing the Best Award Package 114
Assessing Loans as a Factor in the Award Package 116
Assessing Other Cost Factors 116
Negotiating a Better Package 117
Accepting the Award Package 117
Summary 118

19   UNDERSTANDING FEDERAL LOAN REPAYMENT   119

Understanding Your Responsibilities and Rights 119
Deferring Federal Loans 122
Understanding Forbearance 122
Canceling Loans 124
Defaulting on Loans 125
Summary 126

20   PAYING BACK YOUR LOANS   127

How Much Should You Borrow? 127
Estimating Your Future Budget 128
Estimating Loan Payments 130
Can You Afford a Loan? 132
Consolidating Loans 132
Summary 135

APPENDIX A   STATE STUDENT FINANCIAL AID OFFICES   136

APPENDIX B   FINANCIAL AID GLOSSARY   141

INDEX   147

INTRODUCTION

You know that going to graduate school will significantly affect your lifetime earnings. Starting salaries in many fields are far higher for applicants with master's degrees than for those with only bachelor's degrees. And the possibilities for career advancement open up enormously with an advanced degree in hand. However, tuition costs are high and you're probably wary of taking on debt. Can you afford to go?

You know you need to:

- Understand all of the costs associated with going to graduate school.

- Learn what types of aid you're entitled to.

- Analyze how much you need to borrow to complete your studies.

- See how federal low-interest student loans will help fund your education.

- Find out if you're eligible for grants or other awards you don't have to pay back.

To answer your questions, you need the advice and guidance found in the *10 Minute Guide to Paying for Grad School*. Financial planning advice, which is often difficult to obtain, is clearly presented in the proven *10 Minute Guide* no-frills format.

As a potential graduate school applicant, you probably don't have a lot of time to spare. You may still be in college studying for exams, or you may be working a 40-hour week, or at home raising a family. To learn all you need to know, you must make maximum use of your free time. *The 10 Minute Guide to Paying for Grad School* will teach you how to pay for graduate programs in convenient 10-minute lessons.

WHAT IS A 10 MINUTE GUIDE?

The *10 Minute Guide* series is designed to help you accomplish important goals by teaching you the essentials of a subject. Each book offers sound strategies for implementing actions and understanding new materials. In this book, through a series of lessons that take approximately 10 minutes each, you will learn what you must do to finance a graduate education and how and when to apply for financial aid.

USING THIS BOOK

You'll find 20 lessons in this book: each concentrates on one area of the financial aid process. Although you should read through the lessons in the order in which they're presented, you may want to look at Appendix B, "Financial Aid Glossary," before beginning. This glossary will introduce you to the many terms you need to know.

CONVENTIONS USED IN THIS BOOK

The following icons will help you find your way around the *10 Minute Guide to Paying for Grad School:*

 Tip icons signify ideas that cut time and avoid confusion.

 Panic Button icons identify potential problem areas and how to solve them.

 Plain English icons define new terms.

In addition to these icons, the text provides tables, charts, and illustrations to explain key points and simplify complex topics.

Step-by-step instructions are highlighted to simplify complicated procedures.

Using this *10 Minute Guide* is like having your own financial aid adviser behind you. Each lesson gets you closer and closer to funding your education and making your career plans a reality.

Note to the Reader

It's beyond the scope of this book to cover special sources of financial aid for professional schooling. However, the overall financial aid application strategy is the same, and many of the resources cited in this book can be used by professional school applicants. Students interested in professional schooling should contact individual school financial aid and admission offices for information.

For Further Reference

Look for these other Alpha and Arco books that will help you further your graduate school education plans:

- The *10 Minute Guide to Applying to Grad School*, by Sharon McDonnell and Ellen Lichtenstein, 1997, $10.95.

- *GRE: Graduate Record Examination*, by Thomas H. Martinson, 1995, $13.95.

- *GRE SuperCourse*, by Thomas H. Martinson, 1995, $18.95.

- *MAT: Miller Analogies Test*, by William Bader, Daniel S. Burt, and Eve P. Steinberg, 1995, $11.95.

- *TOEFL SuperCourse*, by Grace Yi Qiu Zhong and Patricia Noble Sullivan, 1993, $19.00.

In addition, Arco provides test preparation reviews for individual GRE question types and professional school entrance examinations as well as up-to-date professional school guides.

The Author

Born and raised in New York City, Ellen Lichtenstein received her B.A. at City College of New York. During her publishing career, she has held senior editorial positions with two major publishers and has overseen the development and publication of hundreds of guidance, educational, and consumer reference books for both college and graduate school audiences. She is also the coauthor of the *10 Minute Guide to Applying to Grad School* and the author of the *10 Minute Guide to Building Your Vocabulary*.

Going to Graduate School

In this lesson, you will learn how to evaluate the potential personal and professional advantages of completing a graduate school education.

Benefits of Getting Your Graduate Degree

Increased earnings potential and enhanced career options are two very tangible assets that can come with an advanced degree. There is no denying statistics: In most fields, the more education you have, the better your chances for advancement. However, in fields that are saturated (fields in which there are more job applicants than there are jobs), this may not hold true. You have to research the field(s) you are interested in to discover how much a master's or doctoral degree will benefit your own career goals.

Education and Earnings

There is a direct relationship between educational level and earnings. As shown in Table 1.1, according to the U.S.

Department of Education, between 1980 and 1990 annual income rose more rapidly for persons with higher levels of educational attainment than for those with lower levels.

TABLE 1.1   ANNUAL EARNINGS FOR ADULTS BY LEVEL OF EDUCATION AND SEX

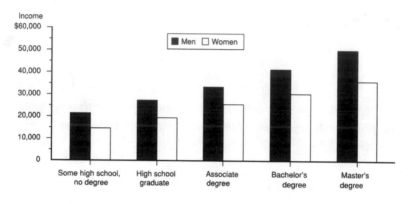

Source: U.S. Department of Education, Digest of Educational Statistics, 1994.

In some careers, there is a definite ceiling on how much you can earn and how far you can advance without a graduate degree. In some specialties, such as teaching or engineering, you can't even begin to build a career without a master's in hand.

EXPLORING YOUR OPTIONS

As you explore the field(s) you are interested in, use all available avenues for research, including public, school, and corporate libraries; friends and colleagues; and human resource professionals. Use the following resources in your research:

- Read government publications. The *Occupational Outlook Handbook* and the *Statistical Abstract* from the U.S. Department of Commerce and the *Digest of*

Educational Statistics from the U.S. Department of Education detail occupational trends, projected salaries, and educational requirements for specific careers.

- Contact professional organizations in the fields that interest you to assess hiring and salary changes. The *Encyclopedia of Associations* (Gale Research) and the *Occupational Outlook Handbook* provide addresses and telephone numbers for professional and trade associations.

- If you are employed, speak to your Human Resources representative to find out your company's policies about employees going for advanced degrees. Ask your supervisor how going to graduate school will affect your career and growth within the company.

- Explore your career skills, likes, and dislikes. The popular paperback *What Color Is Your Parachute?* by Richard Bolles (Ten Speed Press, 1993, $14.95) provides excellent self-tests and checklists for self-assessment. If you want to spend more money and seek professional advice through a career service, you might choose to take career aptitude or career preference tests such as the Strong-Campbell Interest Inventory (SCII) or Career Assessment Inventory (CAI).

WORKING VERSUS GOING TO GRADUATE SCHOOL

If a graduate degree will benefit you, should you go to graduate school immediately after college or wait a few years while you gain work experience? There is no absolute answer. It all depends on your career, finances, and personal ambitions.

ADVANTAGES OF DEFERRING YOUR APPLICATION

By going to work before you apply to graduate school, you have a chance to save money and gain valuable experience that may enhance your studies. Consider your long-term goals and think about the following options:

- Use your earnings from work to set up a graduate school savings program (see Lesson 14). Even if you have a short time horizon before going to graduate school, you can start building your educational nest egg.

- Know what graduate schools look for in their applicants. In some areas of study, graduate schools often prefer students who have had work experience—and thus can bring some real-world learning to their studies—to recent college graduates.

- Know how different employers value graduate degrees. Some companies may reward the older and experienced graduate more handsomely than the rookie who has only an advanced degree and no practical experience to offer.

Students aged 25 and older form the largest segment of the graduate school population.

TABLE 1.2   ENROLLMENT IN GRADUATE SCHOOL BY SELECTED FIELDS OF STUDY AND AGE

FIELD OF STUDY	PERCENTAGE DISTRIBUTION BY AGE		
	UNDER 25	25 TO 35	OVER 35
Accounting	33.2	37.5	29.4
Communications	23.4	49.6	27.0

continues

TABLE 1.2   CONTINUED

| FIELD OF STUDY | PERCENTAGE DISTRIBUTION BY AGE | | |
	UNDER 25	25 TO 35	OVER 35
Computer Science	17.2	57.3	25.5
Economics	25.3	56.0	18.7
Education	11.8	38.2	50.1
Engineering	22.6	63.6	13.9
Liberal Arts	16.1	37.5	46.4
Marketing	37.3	44.8	17.9
Nursing	5.4	38.2	56.4
Political Science	19.0	50.5	30.5
Psychology	21.6	43.1	35.3
Total for All Fields (includes fields not listed)	19.8	48.0	32.2

Source: Adapted from the Digest of Education Statistics, U.S. Department of Education, 1994.

tip   **Serving in the Military**   Serving in the armed forces can offer you excellent educational and financial benefits: The government will pay a large amount of your undergraduate loans; you will be eligible for GI Bill benefits; and you can attend graduate school part-time while in the service and have the government pay 75 percent of the cost. Military service is a serious commitment that may not be right for you or for which you may be ineligible. However, do not hesitate to explore this option. (See information on veterans in Lesson 12.)

SEEKING PRACTICAL ADVICE

Knowing when to go to graduate school may be just as important as making the decision to go in the first place. As mentioned previously, research your field thoroughly. Contact professionals in the field(s) you are interested in and ask them:

- Did they go directly to graduate school after college or did they go to work first?

- If they went directly to graduate school, what advantages or disadvantages did their advanced degree bring to their subsequent career?

- If they worked first, how long did they work before beginning graduate study?

- If they worked first, what advantages or disadvantages did work bring to their graduate study and subsequent career?

- What do representatives from your graduate program of choice think? Ask them for information about the demographic makeup of the student body and for employment and graduation statistics. Many graduate departments offer student counseling and career placement services. Take advantage of them.

SUMMARY

In this lesson, you learned the financial benefits of earning a graduate degree and the advantages of working before applying to graduate school. You also learned about the resources that are available to help you decide if and when to attend graduate school.

UNDERSTANDING YOUR OPTIONS

In this lesson, you will explore the important factors you must consider when selecting a graduate school.

DECIDING BETWEEN FULL- OR PART-TIME STUDY

Will you be one of the growing number of students going to graduate school part-time? Today the number of graduate students enrolled part-time exceeds the number enrolled on a full-time basis. Many working professionals attend graduate school part-time so they can keep their jobs while increasing their skills.

For many students, the desire to get an advanced degree is tempered by the practical reality of having to earn a living. While you may need a graduate degree to advance in your career, you may only be able to afford it by holding down your present job and going to school on a part-time basis.

To see if you're a candidate for part-time study, answer the following questions:

- How long will it take me to complete my degree if I attend graduate school part-time? Will jobs exist for me in my field at graduation?

- Is financial aid available for me if I choose to go to graduate school part-time?

- Will my employer be willing to help finance my education if I study only at night or on weekends? (The greatest source of financial aid for part-time graduate students comes from their employers.)

- Does the school or program I'm interested in offer intensive summer programs or seminars? Can I take time out from my job to attend them?

- Will I be able to manage my course load in addition to my current work and/or family obligations? Will my family and/or employer be supportive? How much time can I devote to school weekly?

- What resources does the graduate school make available to part-time students? What courses are offered? Do part-time students have access to the same professors as full-time students? What are the library hours? What is the availability of counseling and administrative services?

- Will my undergraduate education be considered obsolete if I don't go directly on to graduate school?

Get First-Hand Advice   As you evaluate a graduate school that interests you, try to find out how current part-time students feel about the school and program. Do they feel welcome in the department? Do the professors understand the students' need to balance work and graduate study? How does being a part-time student affect student camaraderie?

UNDERSTANDING YOUR CHOICES

First, know what the benchmark degree is for the field(s) you're interested in—master's or doctoral? Usually, if a doctoral degree is desired, students attend graduate school full-time. In fields in which the master's is the focus, students usually attend graduate school part-time.

The commitments involved in getting advanced degrees at the master's or doctoral level are quite different and should be thoroughly researched by all potential graduate students.

In addition, you sometimes have no choice in deciding between degrees. Some programs require master's degrees before going on for a Ph.D.; other programs or departments don't offer master's degrees.

The choices you must make depend on multiple factors, including your career path, your professional aims, the school and program, financial aid availability, and your personal and family needs.

Master's Degree   An award that requires the successful completion of a program of study of at least the full-time equivalent of one but not more than two years of work beyond the bachelor's degree.

Doctoral Degree   An award that requires work at the graduate level and terminates in a doctoral degree. Currently, the average total time required to attain a Ph.D., including the writing of a dissertation, is over seven years. This figure also includes time to obtain a master's degree.

Now do some arithmetic. How much money do you stand to lose or gain by going to school full-time? Compare the amount of money lost or not earned to your projected earnings after you graduate. (Be realistic—you may not realize your full earning potential until several years after you leave graduate school.) This may dictate that going to school part-time may be your best money-saving strategy.

CHOOSING THE RIGHT SCHOOL

Many factors play a part in selecting the school you will attend. If you're going full-time, academic programs and opportunities should be your first criteria.

If you're going part-time, you want to select the school that offers you the best selection of night and weekend programs. Other factors, such as ease of commute and safety of the campus environs at night, may be very important to the part-time attendee.

ACADEMIC QUALITY OF THE SCHOOL AND PROGRAM

Whether you go full- or part-time, you want to get a good education. But how do you measure quality? The four most-cited factors for assessing quality are faculty, facilities, student body, and reputation. As a potential graduate student, your main concern should be the strength of the program and the department you're interested in—not the school itself. Use the resources in the following list to research the quality of the schools and programs that interest you:

- Study school catalogues and departmental brochures to learn about the department faculty, their education and publications, and which teachers are currently on leave.

- Study departmental course requirements. What are the core requirements, if any, for your program of study? What breadth of courses are offered?

- Get demographic data on student enrollment. How many students are enrolled in the program? What are their backgrounds?

- Find out about the advising program. If you attend the program, will you have a faculty adviser? How will your adviser be chosen? What kind of support can you expect from your adviser?

- Research the size and currency of the school's library holdings.

- Find out about the school's computer resources. Will you have access to free computers and laser printers?

- If you're considering a scientific course of study, find out about the laboratories and research equipment available to you. Will you have access to all the facilities you need?

- Get as much first-hand information as possible. Personal recommendations are your best source of information. If you're still in college, talk to a college placement officer. If you're employed, speak to colleagues or a human resources representative in your company.

- Ask if the school or department issues job placement statistics on its graduates. Many departments prepare their students for the job market by teaching job-hunting techniques.

Set Up an Information-Gathering Deadline You want to know as early as possible which department and faculty is best for you. Your best strategy for finding out about a particular program is to contact the department directly. If you're able to set up an interview with department faculty members, do it. Plan to do this research well in advance of the application process—if possible, one and a half years before enrollment.

COLLEGE COSTS

The costs involved in a graduate education can be substantial. Many students borrow a great deal of money to support their educational goals. How much you can afford is discussed in the following lessons. However, you should not fall into the traps of assuming that expensive tuition and prestigious reputation equals a quality education, or that schools with high tuition offer little financial assistance. When researching costs, don't automatically rule out expensive schools before doing other research. And don't overlook state schools, which often offer resident students the best value for their money (see Lesson 7).

Check Your Alma Mater Don't forget to check out your undergraduate school. If it has a graduate school in your field of study, it might offer great cost incentives to alumni who choose to earn a higher degree. Some universities offer one year of free graduate studies to their former students who graduated with high grade point averages.

OTHER FACTORS TO CONSIDER

Besides academic quality and tuition costs, there are a number of non-academic factors you should consider when choosing a graduate school.

SCHOOL SIZE

As for school size, you must use some discernment. You should focus on what the department you're interested in offers, not on the size of the institution. Don't think in stereotypes. Both large and small schools can offer excellent research facilities, supportive faculty, and an extensive selection of courses. First-hand recommendations may be your best source of information.

LOCATION AND SAFETY

Location is more important than you might think. Know yourself and what environment you feel comfortable in. Both city, suburban, and rural settings have their advantages.

If you plan to attend graduate school full-time, you will need to decide (as you may have done for your undergraduate schooling) how far away from home you want to be. You don't want to add to your stress by putting yourself in uncomfortable surroundings.

However, as a full-time graduate student, your school's location and the environment can significantly affect your studies. Many urban locations offer significant opportunities for research and cultural events. Your likes and dislikes must be weighed accordingly.

If you're considering attending graduate school part-time, you'll most likely have to choose from graduate schools within a convenient commuting distance. But because you will be attending classes at night or on weekends, you should consider the safety of the campus and the commute. Ask yourself the following questions:

- Can I easily commute to the school on nights and weekends? How long will it take me to commute each way?

- Can I take public transportation to school or do I have to drive?

- Does the school offer on-campus parking, or are there inexpensive parking facilities nearby?

- How safe is the area around the campus in the evening?

HOUSING

For full-time students, housing costs and location can be extremely important. Indeed, expenses and quality of housing in urban and non-urban locations vary tremendously across the country. You will want to check out the school's graduate school dorms as well as rentals near the campus. The financial aid administrator should be able to give you helpful information. If you are able to visit the school in advance, you will want to tour on- and off-campus living facilities.

 tip   **Benefits of Living on Campus**   As a graduate student, your work will be draining and sometimes isolating. Living on campus gives you something of a social life. If your school's graduate school dorms are not located on campus, check whether the school has mixed on-campus housing for both graduate and undergraduate students.

Graduate study, whether full- or part-time, is an intense and serious commitment. You'll be at your best in an atmosphere you feel comfortable in.

SUMMARY

In this lesson, you learned about the various factors to consider when choosing a graduate school, including academic programs, cost, size, location, and whether to attend full-time or part-time.

ESTIMATING THE COSTS

In this lesson, you will learn how to add up the costs involved in receiving a graduate school education.

FINANCIAL PLANNING

Going to graduate school means you have to make some serious financial decisions. You must:

1. Know your goals.

2. Understand how much money you need to reach those goals.

3. Figure out how to get the money you need.

Assuming you've decided to go to graduate school, you have to calculate all the costs involved with this commitment. After you do that, you have to realistically assess your current financial worth. Your contribution—how much you can afford to pay—plays a large factor in how much aid you will receive.

 Try Counseling Software If number-crunching intimidates you, you might consider using the Student Loan Counselor financial software developed by Educational Testing Service (ETS) for the Graduate and Professional School Financial Aid Council. Ask a financial aid administrator how you can obtain the program.

Assessing Tuition

While your graduate school costs must be itemized, tuition is usually the first major consideration. Being able to afford tuition is probably the biggest factor in a student's decision to get an advanced degree. While tuition expenses can be substantial, they should not deter you from pursuing your goals. Table 3.1 provides annual tuition ranges for selected graduate and professional programs at private and public universities.

Table 3.1 Average Full-Time Graduate Tuition

	Non-Pro-fessional Programs	Engineering	Medicine	Dentistry	Law
Public*	$3,202	$6,000	$8,768	$8,064	$5,304
Private	$11,079	$17,900	$21,740	$24,318	$16,089

Tuition figures listed for public schools are for state residents. Out-of-state students should budget an additional $1,000–$5,000 for their tuition at public schools.

Source: U.S. Department of Education, Digest of Education Statistics, 1994.

Public versus Private School Tuition Costs
Tuition at public institutions is far more affordable than private universities, especially for resident students. If you're considering attending a public university in another state, find out if you can easily establish residency there. It will save you an enormous amount of money. The best way to learn about residency requirements for a school in another state is to contact the school's financial aid office.

GETTING ACCURATE INFORMATION

Get cost of attendance (budget) figures from the financial aid office of each school you're interested in. You should be able to get a comprehensive breakdown of all costs involved (tuition, fees, books, supplies, and so on), plus an estimate of the average student assistance package for the previous year. The student assistance package is usually divided into two factors:

- Amount of outright awards (money that does not have to be repaid) for the average student

- Amount of loans

Financial Aid Package   This is the total amount of financial aid a student receives, and it includes a combination of federal and nonfederal aid, scholarships, loans, and work-study aid.

Always calculate school-related costs for two or three of your graduate school choices. This may help you make your final graduate school selection.

ESTIMATING PERSONAL EXPENSES

Many students forget that personal expenses, such as car repairs, medical bills, entertainment expenses, and basic necessities, can be exceedingly high. You have to factor in such expenses to avoid underestimating your financial requirements.

 Use Highest Figures Don't underestimate your needs. Rents go up, cars break down, and credit card bills must be repaid. Add a minimum of five percent to your basic personal expense figures to allow for error.

While many schools supply an estimated personal costs figure, assess it carefully and add to it as you see necessary. For more help assessing personal costs, look at the following list of personal and household expenses:

- **Housing Expenses.** Rent or maintenance, mortgage payments, real estate taxes, homeowner's insurance, heat and electricity, water and sewer, and telephone.

- **Food and Beverage Expenses.** Groceries, dining out.

- **Clothes Expenses.** Clothes, shoes, accessories.

- **Household Expenses.** Repair bills, laundry, dry cleaning, housekeeping.

- **Automobile Expenses.** Loans, car insurance, maintenance, repairs, gas.

- **Transportation Expenses.** Commuting costs, tolls, taxis.

- **Medical Expenses.** Medical insurance, doctors, dentists, prescription drugs.

- **Personal Finance Expenses.** Savings, investments, life insurance.

- **Loan Payments.** School loans, credit cards, installment loans.

- **Personal Business Payments.** Payments to accountants or lawyers.

- **Consumer Expenses.** Newspapers, magazines, toiletries.

- **Travel and Entertainment Expenses.** Vacations, movies.

- **Education and Daycare Expenses.** Payments for dependents.

- **Taxes.** Estimated taxes.

- **Miscellaneous.**

These categories were adopted from Department of Commerce classifications.

Using the categories previously listed, estimate your own personal expenses at each graduate school you're considering attending. Add up your figures using the worksheet in Table 3.2.

TABLE 3.2   TOTAL ESTIMATED PERSONAL EXPENSES

TYPE OF EXPENSE	COST
Housing	_____
Food and Beverages	_____
Clothes	_____
Household Operations	_____
Automobile	_____
Transportation	_____
Medical	_____
Personal Finance	_____
Loans	_____
Personal Business	_____
Consumer Goods	_____
Travel and Entertainment	_____
Education and Daycare	_____
Taxes	_____
Miscellaneous	_____
Total Personal Expenses	_____

TOTALING THE COSTS

Now, use Table 3.3 to add up your cost of attendance figures and estimated personal costs. By calculating a budget for one academic year, you will get a rough estimate of your total graduate school costs.

Don't Forget Inflation!   Add seven percent to all tuition costs yearly to allow for inflation.

TABLE 3.3   COST OF ATTENDANCE

TYPE OF EXPENSE	COST
Tuition	_____
Fees	_____
Room and Board	_____
Books and Supplies	_____
Travel	_____
Personal	_____
Total Costs	_____

Use Table 3.3 for every graduate school you're considering to get a sense of what each school will cost you.

SUMMARY

In this lesson, you learned how to estimate the costs of a graduate school education.

4

UNDERSTANDING FINANCIAL AID

In this lesson, you will get a comprehensive overview of financial aid.

SOURCES OF FINANCIAL AID

Financial aid is available from several sources, as shown in the following figure.

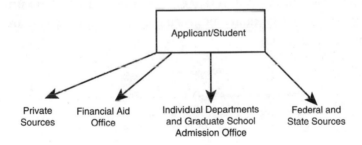

| Applicant/Student |

Private Sources | Financial Aid Office | Individual Departments and Graduate School Admission Office | Federal and State Sources

CLASSIFICATION OF FINANCIAL AID

Much of the funding available to you from government, private, and institutional sources is normally classified as need- or non-need-based aid. Need-based aid is given to students who demonstrate a financial need for assistance; non-need-based aid is awarded for other reasons (such as scholastic achievement). Non-need-based aid includes merit-based and targeted aid.

NEED-BASED AID

A great deal of government and institutional aid is based on student need. How is need determined? The Federal Methodology (FM) formula is used to determine need, and it forms the basis for awarding federal and, in some cases, state aid. It may also be used by universities themselves.

Federal Methodology (FM)   The FM need formula: Cost of Attendance minus Expected Family (Student) Contribution (EFC) equals Financial Need.

There is an important difference in qualifying for federal undergraduate and graduate aid. As a graduate student, you are considered independent.

tip

Need Is Easier to Prove   Because it may be easier to prove financial need at the graduate school level, you should always consider applying for federal financial assistance. But be aware of the dangers of taking on a large amount of debt.

Always check with the financial aid office to find out if any changes have been made in the FM formula. You can also contact the Federal Student Aid Information Center if you have any questions about federal aid. Call or write to:

Federal Student Aid Information Center
P.O. Box 84
Washington, DC 20044
(800) 433-3243

MERIT-BASED AID

Many outright awards such as fellowships, scholarships, and
assistantships are based on merit (usually, high undergraduate
GPAs and standardized test scores). Much merit-based aid
must be thoroughly researched, because aid varies by disci-
pline, school, and private funding source. While some merit-
based awards are intensely competitive, the rewards may be
well worth the trouble of applying (see Lesson 9).

 tip   **Scheduling Test Preparation**   Preparing for standardized tests can be an important strategy in getting merit-based aid, because your test scores may
be used by schools and institutions to determine aid
availability. Set up a study deadline and stick to it.
Take your test early enough to meet all deadlines.

TARGETED AID

Targeted aid is financial aid earmarked for certain groups: students pursuing specific areas of study; minorities and women
under-represented in certain fields; veteran, disabled, and international students; and U.S. students studying overseas. Targeted aid can be need- and non-need-based or even a
combination of the two. Additionally, there are loan programs
set up for specific groups of students, especially students pursuing professional degrees.

FORMS OF FINANCIAL AID

Financial aid is provided in the form of loans, grants, fellow-ships, scholarships, work-study, and assistantships. There are many variations for each aid type. The following list explains the types of financial aid:

- **Loans.** Loans are monies that must be repaid with interest. Educational loans come from government, school, and private sources. Borrowers may be entitled to government low-interest and interest-subsidized loans if they demonstrate financial need.

- **Grants.** Grants are outright awards that do not have to be repaid. Grants are available from government, school, and private sources and may be need-based, merit-based, or targeted aid.

- **Fellowships.** Fellowships are outright awards from public, school, and private sources and do not have to be repaid. Some fellowships have a service component; that is, the applicant has to perform a certain duty or function to receive the award. Fellowships can be need-based, merit-based, or targeted aid.

- **Scholarships.** Scholarships are outright awards from public, school, or private sources that do not have to be repaid. While scholarships are traditionally thought of as merit-based, many scholarships are targeted to certain groups and awarded by financial need.

- **Work-Study.** The term *work-study* is loosely applied to student work arrangements providing employment on- or off-campus, in the private sector, or in non-profit organizations. Federal Work-Study is need-based (see Lesson 8). Internships and coopera-tive education programs are other kinds of work-study arrangements.

- **Assistantships.** Assistantships consist of financial
  aid given for working on campus, usually on a part-
  time basis. Assistantships are usually merit-based,
  although need may be considered in selection. Aid
  may be received in the form of paychecks, tuition
  waivers, or tuition reductions. Teaching, research,
  and administrative assistantships are extremely
  sought-after forms of financial aid.

HOW MANY STUDENTS RECEIVE FINANCIAL AID?

While part-time students often work to support their education or may receive employer assistance, full-time students
need other forms of assistance. Tables 4.1 and 4.2 from the
U.S. Department of Education pinpoint the types and sources
of aid for full- and part-time students.

TABLE 4.1 PERCENTAGE OF GRADUATE STUDENTS RECEIVING AID BY TYPE

	ANY AID	GRANTS	TUITION WAIVERS*	ASSISTANTSHIPS	LOANS	STAFFORD LOANS**
FULL-TIME STUDENTS						
Master's degree	57.6	35.3	12.1	18.6	25.8	23.1
Public	55.1	32.5	15.2	23.4	22.4	19.8
4-yr. non-doctoral	39.3	23.7	6.5	13.0	18.4	16.1
4-yr. doctoral	60.3	35.4	18.0	26.8	23.8	21.1
Private not-for-profit	61.9	40.2	6.8	10.5	31.4	28.7
4-yr. non-doctoral	56.3	35.7	5.0	5.9	30.5	27.5

continues

TABLE **4.1** **CONTINUED**

	ANY AID	GRANTS	TUITION WAIVERS*	ASSISTANTSHIPS	LOANS	STAFFORD LOANS**
FULL-TIME STUDENTS						
4-yr. doctoral	63.7	41.6	7.4	12.0	31.6	29.0
Doctoral degree	74.4	49.1	22.8	37.7	16.1	12.5
Public	72.9	45.2	26.8	42.9	13.7	10.7
Private not-for-profit	77.0	55.8	16.0	28.9	20.3	15.5
PART-TIME STUDENTS						
Master's degree	32.6	24.7	5.7	4.3	6.0	5.3
Public	27.0	19.0	5.6	5.3	5.1	4.6
4-yr. non-doctoral	23.6	17.1	5.3	3.0	4.5	3.9
4-yr. doctoral	29.1	20.3	5.8	6.8	5.5	5.0
Private not-for-profit	43.1	35.3	5.8	2.5	7.7	6.6
4-yr. non-doctoral	37.7	31.6	5.0	1.4	5.9	5.1
4-yr. doctoral	46.7	37.7	6.3	3.3	8.8	7.5
Doctoral degree	43.9	30.3	15.6	19.7	6.2	4.8
Public	42.8	29.0	17.6	22.5	5.7	4.5
Private not-for-profit	47.8	35.2	7.9	9.0	8.0	6.1

Included in Grants column as well.
**Included in Loans column as well.*
Source: National Center for Education Statistics, Statistical Analysis Report, 1993.

TABLE 4.2   PERCENTAGE OF GRADUATE STUDENTS RECEIVING AID BY SOURCE OF AID

	ANY AID	FEDERAL	STATE	SCHOOL	OTHER*	EMPLOYER**
FULL-TIME STUDENTS						
Master's degree	57.6	25.6	4.7	37.2	12.5	6.4
Public	55.1	22.5	5.8	38.6	9.4	4.6
4-yr. non-doctoral	39.3	17.9	9.3	20.1	8.2	4.8
4-yr. doctoral	60.3	24.0	4.6	44.7	9.7	4.5
Private not-for-profit	61.9	30.9	2.7	34.7	17.8	9.4
4-yr. non-doctoral	56.3	30.5	3.8	28.2	18.2	8.8
4-yr. doctoral	63.7	31.1	2.4	36.7	17.7	9.6
Doctoral degree	74.4	17.5	6.1	65.9	16.5	6.0
Public	72.9	15.1	7.8	65.0	18.2	7.0
Private not-for-profit	77.0	21.6	3.3	67.5	13.5	4.3
PART-TIME STUDENTS						
Master's degree	32.6	6.2	1.0	13.1	18.5	15.4
Public	27.0	5.3	1.0	12.3	14.4	11.4
4-yr. non-doctoral	23.6	5.0	1.2	9.5	13.5	10.6
4-yr. doctoral	29.1	5.5	0.9	14.0	15.1	11.9
Private not-for-profit	43.1	7.9	1.0	14.5	26.1	23.0
4-yr. non-doctoral	37.7	6.3	1.9	13.0	22.3	18.6
4-yr. doctoral	46.7	9.0	0.3	15.5	28.6	25.9
Doctoral degree	43.9	5.3	1.6	33.5	16.3	9.7
Public	42.8	5.1	2.0	35.9	14.1	7.4
Private not-for-profit	47.8	6.1	0.0	24.7	24.7	18.4

Includes all sources of aid other than federal, state, or school. Examples of other sources are corporations, unions, foundations, fraternal organizations, and community organizations.
**Included in Other column as well.*
Source: National Center for Education Statistics, Statistical Analysis Report, 1993.

Give Yourself Time   The more time you have for research, the better. Ideally, you should start seeking funding sources one to one-and-a-half years before you apply to graduate school.

SUMMARY

In this lesson, you learned the basics of the types and sources of financial aid.

Understanding Federal Loans

In this lesson, you will learn about federal loan programs for graduate study, including the three most common forms of federal aid available: Perkins Loans, Subsidized Stafford Loans, and Unsubsidized Stafford Loans.

Borrowing from Your Uncle

Federal loans for graduate study currently exceed four billion dollars, a figure which is expected to increase. While certain features of federal student loans may change in the near future, their favorable low interest rates will continue to make them the best loan sources available.

To qualify for federal aid, students must be U.S. citizens or eligible non-citizens (for example, permanent residents and certain refugees).

You can apply for all federal loans with the Free Application for Federal Student Aid (FAFSA) form. See Lesson 16 for more information on completing this form.

Getting Information   Your primary source of loan information should be your school's financial aid office. However, you can also obtain basic information about federal aid from the U.S. Department of Education at (800) 4-FED AID (433-3243) or (800) 730-8913 for the hearing impaired.

PERKINS LOANS

Federal Perkins Loans are directly administered through colleges. A financial aid administrator can tell you whether a specific school participates in the Perkins Loan program. The following list explains the Perkins Loan program in more detail:

- **Eligibility.** Students with exceptional financial need who are enrolled in a participating school and who need a loan to meet their educational expenses are considered. Applicants must be U.S. citizens or eligible non-citizens.

- **Loan Amount.** The total amount you can borrow for graduate study is $30,000. (Totals include all previous Perkins Loans. Under certain circumstances, you may be able to borrow more money. Ask your financial aid officer for more information.)

- **Interest Rate.** The low-interest rate is 5 percent.

- **Repayment Schedule.** Repayments begin six to nine months after you leave school, with up to ten years to repay.

- **Fees.** You are not charged origination or insurance premium fees.

Loan Fees   When you borrow money, you are normally charged certain fees by the lender. Common loan fees include origination fees (for processing the loan) or insurance premium fees (for guaranteeing the loan). Both fees are usually deducted from the dollar amount of the loan before you receive your money.

Table 5.1 shows repayments on Perkins Loans.

TABLE 5.1   TYPICAL PAYMENTS ON PERKINS LOANS

TOTAL LOAN AMOUNT	NUMBER OF PAYMENTS	MONTHLY PAYMENT	TOTAL INTEREST CHARGES	TOTAL REPAID
$3,000	119	$31.84	$817.86	$3,817.86
	1	$28.90		
$5,000	119	$53.06	$1,363.40	$6363.40
	1	$49.26		
$15,000	119	$159.16	$4,090.85	$19,090.85
	1	$150.81		

Because Perkins Loans are the most attractive of the three major federal loans, their availability may be a consideration when you apply to graduate school.

STAFFORD LOAN PROGRAM

Stafford loans are administered through the following two federal programs:

- Federal Direct Student Loan (Direct Loan) Program

- Federal Family Education Loan (FFEL) Program

The difference between the two programs is in the lender. With Direct Loans, the federal government makes loans directly to students through schools. Under the FFEL Program, a private lender makes the loan, but the government guarantees that it will be repaid.

 Private Lender   Private lenders are non-governmental loan sources and include commercial lenders (such as banks, savings and loans, and credit unions), private loan programs (see Lesson 6), and schools.

In terms of payments, the most important difference between the two programs is the loan repayment schedule. For Direct Loans, you have several repayment options and can have as many as 30 years to make repayment (depending on the repayment plan and the amount of money you borrowed). Under FFEL, you are required to repay the loan within 10 years.

Your school's financial aid officer can tell you which program(s) the school participates in. Ask about all options, but remember—the longer the repayment schedule, the more interest you will pay.

 Finding Stafford Loan Lenders   Ask your school or state financial aid officer for recommended lenders. It pays to shop around.

SUBSIDIZED STAFFORD LOANS

Subsidized Stafford Loans (formerly Guaranteed Student Loans) are available through participating commercial and savings banks, savings and loan associations, credit unions, finance companies, and institutions (under the Direct Loan Program). Although their interest rate is higher than Perkins Loans, they are still better than many other loans because of their federal guarantee.

The following list explains the guidelines of the Subsidized Stafford Loan Program in more detail.

- **Eligibility.** Graduate students are eligible if they demonstrate financial need, are enrolled at least half-time at an eligible educational institution, are making satisfactory academic progress toward a degree, and are U.S. citizens or eligible non-citizens. Students cannot borrow more than their cost of attendance minus any other financial aid for which they are eligible.

- **Loan Amount.** Students can borrow up to $8,500 per academic year with a cumulative amount of $65,500. (This amount includes any benefits received as an undergraduate.)

- **Interest Rate.** The variable interest rate, currently capped (held at a maximum) at 7.66 percent, is reset annually.

- **Repayment Schedule.** Currently, students have a six-month grace period after graduation before they have to start repaying the loan. The government pays the interest on these loans while you are in school, during the grace period, and during deferment periods.

- **Fees.** There is a 4 percent fee (3 percent origination plus 1 percent insurance) charged for each loan disbursement.

 Fees Add Up While a 4 percent fee may seem high, private loan origination fees can run far higher. This is a positive feature of the Stafford Loan Program. Be certain you don't incur additional fees during repayment by not paying on time.

Unsubsidized Stafford Loans

Non-need-based Unsubsidized Stafford Loans, while not as attractive as the previous two options, provide another low-interest source for borrowing. The following list explains the guidelines of Unsubsidized Stafford Loans in more detail.

- **Eligibility.** The same as for subsidized Stafford Loans; however, financial need is not a factor.

- **Loan Amount.** Students may borrow up to $10,000 per academic year to a cumulative total of $138,500. (This total includes subsidized and unsubsidized Stafford Loans for both graduate and undergraduate study.) Thus, the maximum loan amounts for a graduate student each year are: $8,500 (subsidized) + $10,000 (unsubsidized) = $18,500. The maximum aggregate loan amount for Stafford Loans (subsidized and unsubsidized) is $138,500, with a $65,500 cap on the subsidized loan.

- **Interest Rate.** The interest rate is the same as for subsidized Stafford Loans.

- **Repayment Schedule.** There is no interest subsidy. Borrowers must begin interest payments immediately unless the lender agrees to accrue interest during enrollment.

- **Fees.** Fees are the same as for subsidized Stafford Loans.

TABLE 5.2 TYPICAL 10-YEAR STAFFORD LOAN FIXED REPAYMENT SCHEDULE

TOTAL LOAN AMOUNT	NUMBER OF PAYMENTS	MONTHLY PAYMENT	TOTAL INTEREST CHARGES	TOTAL REPAID
$2,600	65	$50.00	$628.42	$3,228.42
$4,000	120	$49.06	$1,887.20	$5,887.20
$7,500	120	$91.99	$3,538.80	$11,038.80
$10,000	120	$122.65	$4,718.00	$14,718.00
$15,000	120	$183.98	$7,077.60	$22,077.60

Source: U.S. Department of Education, Student Guide to Financial Aid, 1995-1996.

While borrowers may allow the interest to accumulate on unsubsidized loans, you will pay less if you pay the interest off immediately. If you allow interest to accumulate, it will be capitalized (added to the principal amount of the loan). This will increase the total amount you have to repay.

Never Capitalize Quarterly! If you choose to defer and capitalize interest on Unsubsidized Stafford Loans, you will save money by finding a lender who capitalizes interest at repayment. The most expensive method of capitalizing is quarterly, followed by semi-annually and annually. Capitalizing at repayment is your least expensive option since there is less accrued interest to repay.

If you know you need to borrow money, give yourself as much time as possible to seek out and compare lenders. This is the case for all loans—government and private.

SUMMARY

In this lesson, you learned the advantages and disadvantages of the three most common federal loan programs: Perkins Loans, Subsidized Stafford Loans, and Unsubsidized Stafford Loans.

SEEKING PRIVATE LOANS AND ALTERNATIVE FUNDING

In this lesson, you will learn how to find loans from commercial, school, or other private lenders, as well as alternative funding sources such as employer assistance.

GOING THE PRIVATE FUNDING ROUTE

If you're unable to qualify for government loans (which are often based on need), a private loan may be your best option. This is especially true for students who work full-time. You may also need a loan to make up the unmet needs not covered in your financial aid package.

tip

Shop Around for Deals As soon as you consider going to graduate school, check out loan availability from commercial sources such as banks, savings and loans, credit unions, and

continues

finance companies. While you should *not* apply for these loans before you need to, early research will save you time later on.

Your aim is to find the loans that offer the lowest interest rates and borrowing charges (including origination and insurance/guarantee fees). While interest rates on federal loans are capped, interest rates on private loans are not. Many lenders offer several loan programs that feature different repayment schedules and interest terms. You will have to determine which one is best for you.

Taking Out a Home Equity Loan   If you own your own home and have equity in it, a home equity loan may be an attractive option, especially at a time when interest rates are low. Look for home equity loans with no closing fees and the lowest charges. Remember—interest charged on home equity loans is usually tax-deductible.

Ask Your Own Bank for Better Terms   If you're borrowing a substantial amount of money and have a long-established relationship with a particular bank, don't hesitate to ask the bank for better loan rates. This can mean lower interest rates or lower fees on personal and home equity loans. Before doing this, make sure you have a good credit rating, then shop around to find out what other banks charge. When you negotiate with your bank, ask the loan officer to beat the best deals offered.

SPECIAL PRIVATE PROGRAMS

There are several attractive loan programs available to credit-worthy graduate students and to students whose eligibility is based on future earnings potential. Contact the following sources for information on special loan programs:

TERI Alternative Loan Programs and Professional
  Education Plan (PEP)
The Education Resources Institute (TERI)
330 Stuart Avenue, Suite 500
Boston, MA 02116-5237
(800) 255-8374

Option 4 Loan Program
USA Funds
Option 4 Loan Program
P.O. Box 6198
Indianapolis, IN 46206-6198
(800) 635-3785

AchieverLoan
Knight College Resource Group
855 Boyston Street
Boston, MA 02116
(800) 255-6783

GradEXCEL and GradSHARE
New England Education Loan Marketing Corp.
(Nellie Mae)
50 Braintree Hill Park, Suite 300
Braintree, MA 02184
(800) 634-9308

Check with Nellie Mae. The Nellie Mae program currently has a special loan available at universities. The loan features low default rates in which Nellie Mae pays the 1 percent guarantee fee on the borrower's behalf.

SCHOOL PROGRAMS

Check with a financial aid administrator to see if your school offers the following:

- No-interest monthly payment plans for tuition and room and board. This may be a better option for you than having to make large lump-sum payments.

- Private low-interest loan payment programs. Often, such programs are used to meet the needs of students who applied too late to qualify for financial aid.

FUNDING THROUGH YOUR JOB

If you're employed, find out whether your company is willing to help fund your education. Ask your supervisor or Human Resources representative about company policy. Employee tuition benefits often go unused because people are unaware of their availability.

Employee Tuition Assistance is Taxable for Graduate Study   Nearly all employee tuition benefits are taxable; tuition reimbursement is classified as taxable income. If you want to avoid paying taxes on your tuition assistance, your courses must qualify as a business expense, which means they must be necessary for you to do your current work—*not* to obtain a promotion. Ask a Human Resources or Payroll representative how tuition assistance will affect your take-home pay.

If you have a credit union at work or through your union, check out its terms for private and home equity loans. Credit unions often have far more attractive loan policies and charge lower fees than banks or savings and loans.

Contact the Credit Union National Association (CUNA) for information on finding and joining a credit union. CUNA can be reached by phone at (800) 358-5710. Or, you can find CUNA's home page on the World Wide Web at http://www.cuna.org.

Borrowing from Your 401(k)   Caution! If you participate in a company 401(k) retirement savings program, consider all other options before you borrow from it. Although you may be able to borrow without penalty, this money should be reserved for your retirement funding. Also, if you leave or lose your job before you repay the loan, you must repay the loan balance within 30 days to avoid paying federal income tax on the amount you owe.

Finding Part-Time Work

Working in accordance with traditional work-study arrangements (see Lesson 8) or finding outside part-time employment are other options. At the very least, part-time work will help pay for basic expenses and can provide a cushion in case of emergencies. Check with the school financial aid office and student employment office for on- and off-campus employment opportunities.

Working Full-Time for a University   Some universities offer full-time employees partial or full tuition waivers. For part-time students, this is an excellent opportunity to make school contacts that could pave the way for outright financial awards. As stated previously, these benefits are taxed.

SUMMARY

In this lesson, you learned about private and school loan sources, as well as employee assistance programs.

DISCOVERING FINANCIAL AID FROM STATE SOURCES

In this lesson, you will explore state government sources of financial aid, which are often overlooked by graduate students seeking funding.

EXPLORING ALL OPTIONS

Both need- and non-need-based funding may be available in your state in the form of loans, grants, scholarships, and other awards. While such money may be limited to state residents who are attending graduate school in-state, this is not always the case. Some states have reciprocal study arrangements with other states. Other programs may be open to out-of-state students. You must research this option.

> **tip** **Need May Be Easier to Prove** Some states use different formulas for assessing financial aid than the federal government. Therefore, it may be easier for you to obtain state aid. Never assume you will be disqualified before you research your state's guidelines.

Contact your state student financial aid office directly (see Appendix A). Your school financial aid office should also be able to supply you with information on state financial assistance programs.

STATE LOANS

State educational loans are probably a better value than commercial and private loans. Additionally, there are loan forgiveness or cancellation programs in many states for such professions as nursing and teaching.

Loan Forgiveness (Cancellation) Programs
Programs in which the lender forgives your loan based on your activities after graduation. To find out about your state's policies, contact your state student financial aid office (see Appendix A) or your school's financial aid office.

MATCHING STUDENT GRANTS

The U.S. Department of Education provides some states with funding to match student grant programs. Contact your state's student financial aid office (see Appendix A) as early as possible to inquire about such funding.

As you contact state financial aid departments to find out what funding opportunities are available, you might want to use the following questionnaire as a guideline.

Y	N	Do I meet state residency requirements for state aid?
Y	N	If not, can I meet requirements with short-term residency?
Y	N	Do I know what formula the state uses to calculate financial need?
Y	N	Is financial aid administered by the state?
Y	N	Is financial aid administered by the university?
Y	N	Does the state have special loan programs?
Y	N	Does the state have any policy to forgive loans in my field?
Y	N	Does the state participate in any matching fund programs?
Y	N	Do I have all application forms and deadline information?

 Public Ivys   This term refers to state universities, which often are an excellent financial value for in-state residents. In many cases, state universities offer outstanding educational programs.

SUMMARY

In this lesson, you learned about state sources of aid.

8

FEDERAL WORK-STUDY (FWS) AND OTHER WORK PROGRAMS

In this lesson, you will learn about government, institutional, and private service-related programs.

FEDERAL WORK-STUDY (FWS)

Under this program, students with financial need are given jobs so they can earn money to pay for their educational expenses. The FWS program encourages community-service work and work related to your course of study. Usually, FWS recipients work at public and private nonprofit organizations. However, some schools have agreements with private non-profit employers for FWS jobs, which must be relevant to the FWS recipients' line of study.

FWS is a campus-based program administered by the financial aid office of participating schools. You can apply for this program by filling out the FAFSA application (see Lesson 16).

Federal Work-Study (FWS) is available to students who meet the following requirements:

- Demonstrate financial need

- Are enrolled in participating institutions

- Are U.S. citizens or eligible non-citizens

While the wages you earn in the FWS program will probably vary depending on the type of work you do, the scale will be low but not lower than the current federal minimum wage. However, the amount you earn can't exceed your total FWS award. When assigning work hours, your employer or the financial aid administrator will consider your class schedule and academic progress.

Finding Work-Study Jobs   Consult your school financial aid administrator on how you must conduct your job search. Your job hiring must be cleared with the school financial aid office.

FWS can be a valuable part of your education if you find work allied to your course of study. Work with the financial aid administrator to find jobs that serve your needs. Because the payment of wages under FWS is shared between the federal government and the employer, many research programs can stretch their grants by hiring work-study students. You may be able to find coveted research or teaching assistantships through this program.

Deadlines Count   Each school sets its own deadlines for campus-based FWS programs. The deadlines will usually be earlier than the U.S. Department of Education's deadline for filing a federal student financial aid application. Make sure you know your school's deadline.

ASSISTANTSHIPS

Assistantships are a valuable source of financial aid for graduate students. Many assistantships offer students a great opportunity to either teach or do research in their fields. While most assistantships are awarded on the basis of merit, need may be taken into account.

Financial aid from assistantships can be offered in the form of:

- Tuition waivers

- Tuition waivers plus stipends

- Stipends alone

 Stipends   For graduate students, a stipend most often refers to the salary given to teaching, research, and administrative assistants.

In addition, the terms and awarding of assistantships will differ from school to school. Assistantships may be restricted as follows:

- Earmarked for only the first year of graduate study or prohibited to first-year students

- Annually renewable upon application and evidence of satisfactory work

- Guaranteed for a specified number of years

The following list explains the different kinds of assistantships available.

- **Teaching Assistantships (TAs).** TAs help professors read and grade papers, run small seminars, and tutor small groups.

- **Research Assistantships (RAs).** RAs help professors do research, carry out experiments, and analyze data. RA positions are common in science-related departments.

- **Administrative Assistantships.** Administrative assistants provide supporting services to specific departments. The nature of the work can vary greatly—from purely clerical functions to jobs allied to academic interests.

- **Residence Assistantships.** Residence assistants help out in undergraduate dormitories. They often receive free room and board for their services.

APPLYING FOR ASSISTANTSHIPS

To learn about and apply for an assistantship, go to the department, the graduate admission office, and the financial aid office.

Teaching and research assistantships are highly prized and competition to get them is often fierce. Because these awards are often awarded by the department, you should seek out potential faculty advisors or interview faculty as early as possible—even when you are choosing a graduate school.

SERVICE-RELATED GRANTS AND FELLOWSHIPS

Some fellowships or grants have a service requirement. For example, they may require recipients to carry out specific research. These awards come from institutional, governmental, or private sources. You can find out about such aid through the financial aid office, graduate admission office, your department, or your own research.

COOPERATIVE EDUCATION

Cooperative education programs offer a combined work-study arrangement in which you may earn academic credit for your work. A financial aid administrator will be able to tell you about the school's programs.

If you work, ask a Human Resources representative if your employer has such programs with specific schools. To explore cooperative education, contact:

> National Center for Cooperative Education
> Northeastern University
> 360 Huntington Avenue
> Boston, MA 02115
> (617) 437-3778

INTERNSHIPS

Both paid and unpaid internships offer students the opportunity to work with participating organizations outside of school, usually while gaining academic credit. You can find out if your school has internship programs through the financial aid office or the department.

tip

Other Employment If you are unable to qualify for a service-related program and you need additional funds, you should consider part-time work. Ask staff at the financial aid office and student employment center for suggestions.

Are They Taxable? All students receiving service-related awards must check with the financial aid office to see how their awards should be reported for tax purposes.

SUMMARY

In this lesson, you learned about service-related programs, including Federal Work-Study, assistantships, cooperative education, internships, and other employment.

Seeking Out Private Grants, Fellowships, and Scholarships

*In this lesson, you will learn how to obtain outright funding—
money you don't have to repay.*

Understanding the Types and Sources of Outright Awards

Many sources of private funding exist. However, many gifts
are not awarded because students do not apply for them. The
following lists the sources of outright awards:

- Foundations

- Corporations and unions

- Professional and educational associations

- Sororities and fraternities

- Civic and religious groups

- Cultural and ethnic associations

- Schools or institutions

Outright awards from private sources can be need-based, merit-based, or a combination of the two. However, 80 percent of these awards from private sector sources do not require you to submit financial statements or demonstrate financial need.

While some awards are granted for general graduate study, most are aimed at students in particular academic fields or specific areas of research.

Exploring Available Funding Sources

Sizable awards exist at both the master's and doctoral levels. It's up to you to discover funding sources by doing the necessary research. Sources of information include your school, the library, the Internet and World Wide Web, the Foundation Center, private scholarship search firms, bookstores, and specific award programs.

Using Your School

First, check out all suggested funding sources from your school's financial aid office, office of graduate school admission, and your individual department. Some graduate programs may have a designated grants officer to help you.

While your financial aid application will put you in the running for school awards, you can increase your chances of receiving awards by making strong faculty contacts. If you can't do this before applying, do it during your first year in graduate school. Remember to go directly to your department, as well as to the graduate school admission office and the school financial aid office when you research institutional aid.

High Tuition, Large Endowments Expensive schools may have large endowments (private donations to the college) which can translate into aid money in the form of grants and scholarships. Ask a school financial aid officer about possible grants and scholarships available in your field or area of research.

USING THE LIBRARY

Go to your public, school, or corporate library for research. The following annual directories are excellent references for researching private funding:

- *Scholarships, Fellowships, and Loans*, published by Gale Research

- *Annual Register of Grant Support*, published by R. R. Bowker

- *The Grants Register 1995-1997*, published by St. Martin's Press

- *The Foundation Directory*, published by the Foundation Center

- *National Directory of Corporate Giving*, published by the Foundation Center

USING A COMPUTER

Online information resources are available for exploring private funding. Contact the following recommended sources for more information concerning costs:

- *The Foundation Directory* contains descriptions of more than 34,000 active grant-making foundations.

The Foundation Center
79 Fifth Avenue
New York, NY 10003-3050
(212) 620-4230
Fax: (212) 691-1828
Online: DIALOG (Knight-Ridder Information Services, Inc.)

- *Grants* offers information on more than 8,700 grant sources in the arts, humanities, sciences, and social sciences.

Oryx Press
4041 North Central Avenue
Phoenix, AZ 85012-2397
(602) 265-2651; (800) 279-6799
Fax: (602) 265-6250
E-mail: info@orxypress.com (Internet)
Online: DIALOG (Knight-Ridder Information Services, Inc.); also available on CD-ROM

Free Online Search   On the World Wide Web, you can use a free computerized scholarship service from Student Services Inc. and Student Aid Research Through Technology. Within 15 minutes of completing a questionnaire, you will receive a customized list of financial aid sources via e-mail.

site: fastWeb

location: http://web.studentservices.com/fastweb

Using the Foundation Center Libraries

The Foundation Center maintains four full-scale libraries where librarians can help you seek funding information. In addition to the New York center (listed in the previous section), the locations are:

312 Sutter Street
San Francisco, CA 94108
(415) 397-0902

1001 Connecticut Avenue, NW, Suite 938
Washington, DC 20036
(202) 331-1400

1422 Euclid Avenue
Cleveland, OH 44115
(216) 861-1934

Using Private Scholarship Search Firms

Consider researching outright awards through a private scholarship search firm, which may provide a more thorough search for funding than your individual efforts. Contact the following for more information:

National Scholarship Research Service
P.O. Box 6609
Santa Rosa, CA 95406-0609
(707) 546-6777

Be Wary of Scholarship Search Firms   Always watch out for firms that charge high fees and offer no refunds. Scholarship search firms often provide the same information you can obtain yourself with a little time and effort.

USING THE BOOKSTORE

The following publications are readily available in large bookstores:

- *Free Money for Graduate School*, by Laurie Blum, Henry Holt & Company, 1994, $12.95. This is an excellent compendium of more than 1,000 grants, fellowships, and scholarships for graduate study.

- *Worldwide Graduate Scholarship Directory*, 4th ed., by Dan Cassidy, Career Press, 1995, $26.99. This is a comprehensive and up-to-date source of outright awards derived from the National Scholarship Research Service (NSRS) database.

USING AWARD PROGRAMS

The following award programs are excellent and prestigious sources of graduate school support:

British Marshall Scholarships
Marshall Aid Commemoration Commission
British Embassy
3100 Massachusetts Avenue, NW
Washington, DC 20008
(202) 462-1340
Deadline: mid-October

Getty Pre-doctoral Fellowships
Getty Center for the History of Art and the Humanities
401 Wilshire Boulevard
Santa Monica, CA 90401
(301) 458-9811
Deadline: December 1

Hertz Fellowships in the Applied Physical Sciences
Fannie and John Hertz Foundation
P.O. Box 5032
Livermore, CA 94551-5032
(510) 373-1642
Deadline: mid-October

Lindbergh Grants Program
Charles A. Lindbergh Fund
708 East Third Street
Minneapolis, MN 55415
(612) 338-1703
Deadline: mid-June

Mellon Fellowships in Humanistic Studies
Woodrow Wilson National Fellowship Foundation
CN 5329
Princeton, NJ 08542-5329
(609) 452-7007
Nomination deadline: early November
Application deadline: late November

Space Industrialization Fellowships
Space Foundation
4800 Research Forest Drive
Woodlands, TX 77381
(713) 363-7944
Deadline: early October

Applying for Outright Awards Applying for outright awards may take a great deal of work (see Lesson 11); however, the rewards can justify your effort. Many graduate-level awards are sizable—some fellowships can cover your entire tuition. Another plus: Many awards are renewable. You do not have to reapply each year!

HOW AWARDS AFFECT FINANCIAL AID ELIGIBILITY

Federal regulations mandate that awards from sources outside the institution be treated as educational resources for determining your eligibility for financial aid. Many schools use such resources to first reduce unmet need, then loan eligibility, then work eligibility, and finally, school scholarships, fellowships, or grants.

Ask each school about its methods. But do not avoid applying for outright awards because of their effect on your financial aid package.

  Taxes on Awards   Regarding taxes on outright awards, some of it may be taxable, even if you do not receive a W-2. For degree candidates, amounts used for expenses other than tuition and coursework are taxable.

SUMMARY

In this lesson, you learned about the many resources through which you can discover sources of private grants, fellowships, and scholarships

RESEARCHING FEDERAL GRANTS

In this lesson, you will learn how to research and seek out federal grants, fellowships, and scholarships—money that doesn't have to be repaid.

DOING YOUR HOMEWORK

The secret to finding grant money is to thoroughly explore all the programs that offer it. In fact, a great deal of money available for graduate study goes unclaimed because students don't know it's availabile. It's not just the Department of Education that provides educational funding. You should research other federal agencies, including those shown in Figure 10.1, for award possibilities.

Use all of the resources available to you including the financial aid office, the graduate admission office, and individual departments. Your graduate school may have a dedicated grants officer to help you.

tip   **Most Lucrative Awards**   While there are government grants available in all areas of study, many of the most lucrative government awards are in science and engineering.

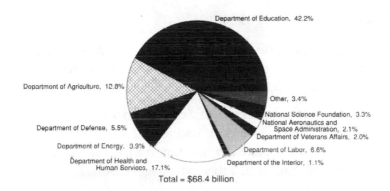

Figure 10.1   Federal funds for education by agency.

Source: U.S. Office of Management and Budget, Budget of the U.S. Government, Fiscal Year 1995; and National Science Foundation, Federal Funds for Research and Development, Fiscal Years 1992, 1993, and 1994.

 Application Deadlines   Get all the award application information you need as early as possible. Submitting accurate and well-thought-out applications and adhering to deadlines is crucial. Read Lesson 11 for advice on preparing grant applications.

RESEARCHING ALL SOURCES

In the following sections, you explore all possible avenues of federal grants, fellowships, and scholarships, including computer listings, library references, and specific award programs.

USING ONLINE RESOURCES

Information resources are available online for researching federal awards. Contact the following sources for more information:

- **Computer Retrieval of Information on Scientific Projects (CRISP).** Includes grants and awards funded by the National Institutes of Health (NIH) and other public health services agencies.

  U.S. National Institutes of Health
  Division of Research Grants
  Research Documentation Section
  5333 Westbard Avenue
  Bethesda, MD 20892
  (301) 594-7267
  Fax: (301) 594-8226
  Online: CDP Online (also available on CD-ROM)

- **Federal Assistance Programs Retrieval System (FAPRS).** Includes information on government loans programs, grants, and scholarships.

  U.S. General Services Administration
  Federal Domestic Assistance Catalog Staff
  300 Seventh Avenue, SW
  Washington, DC 20407
  (202) 708-5126
  Fax: (202) 401-8233
  Online: U.S. General Services Administration, Federal Domestic Assistance Catalog Staff; CARL Systems Network (also available on disk)

- **Lesko's Info-Power.** Includes information on government grants for higher education.

Information USA, Inc.
P.O. Box E
Kennsington, MD 20895
(301) 924-0556; (800) 955-7963
Fax: (301) 924-1639
Online: CompuServe (also available on CD-ROM and
   on disk)

tip

Researching on the Internet If you have access
to the Internet, check out the Grant Getter's Guide
to the Internet, sponsored by the University of
Idaho. This service provides a summary of
Internet-accessible information on federal grants
from many government agencies. For more information, contact James Kearny at jkearney@
ravencsrv.uidaho.edu or Marty Zimmerman at
marty@uidaho.edu.

USING THE LIBRARY

In addition to the resources listed in Lesson 9, you should look
for the following references at your library:

- *Catalog of Federal Domestic Assistance*, published by
  the U.S. Government Printing Office. Contains comprehensive descriptions of individual agency assistance programs.

- *Government Assistance Almanac*, by J. Robert
  Dumouchel, Omnigraphics, 1994. Complete guide
  to federal programs, including student aid.

- *Lesko's Info-Power*, by Matthew Lesko, Gale Research,
  1993.

- *Using Government Information Sources,* by Jean L. Sears and Marilyn K. Moody, Oryx Press, 1994. Provides in-depth guidance on how to research government information. Has an excellent bibliography of source materials on grants.

USING SPECIFIC PROGRAMS

The following awards are considered excellent and prestigious sources of financial aid:

Jacob K. Javits Fellowships
(arts, humanities, and social science)
U.S. Department of Education
400 Maryland Avenue, SW, Portals C-80, MS 5251
Washington, DC 20202-5251
(202) 260-2574
Deadline: late November

National Aeronautics and Space Administration (NASA)
Graduate Student Researchers Program
NASA, Higher Education Branch—Code FEH
Washington, DC 20546
(202) 358-1531
Deadline: February 1

National Defense Science and Engineering Fellowships
NDSEG Fellowship Program
200 Park Drive, Suite 21
P.O. Box 13444
Research Triangle Park, NC 27709-3444
(919) 549-8505
Deadline: early January

National Institute of Health Training Grants
NIH, Division of Research and Training Grants
533 Westbard Avenue
Bethesda, MD 20892
(301) 496-7441

National Science Foundation Fellowships
(minority and non-minority competition)
Oak Ridge Associated Universities
P.O. Box 3010
Oak Ridge, TN 37831-3010
(615) 241-4300

 tip **Studying Abroad**   To learn about the Fulbright award programs sponsored by the U.S. Department of Education, contact:

Fulbright U.S. Graduate Student Program
Institute of International Education
809 United Nations Plaza
New York, NY 10017
(212) 984-5330

SUMMARY

In this chapter, you learned about various sources of information on federal grants, fellowships, and scholarships.

PREPARING GRANT APPLICATIONS

In this lesson, you will explore basic grant application and proposal writing procedures.

APPLICATION PROCEDURES

Different awards call for different application procedures—from filling out simple applications and writing short essays to preparing lengthy proposals. Federal awards will probably call for filling out many forms. However, most of the awards at the master's level will call for a simple personal statement or essay, not a full-blown proposal.

> **tip** **Getting Help from Your School** You should seek the help of your school and your department if you have questions concerning an application. Remember, if there's a grants officer in the graduate program, ask him or her for assistance.

As soon as you locate awards you want to apply for, contact the sponsors to get information and application requirements. The following is a list of possible grant requirements:

- One to two essays or personal statements

- Personal interviews

- Personal letters of recommendation

- Resume or curriculum vitae

- College academic and financial transcripts

- Undergraduate and graduate school standardized entrance examination scores

- Copies of your most recent tax return (and possibly your parents') when demonstrating need

- A detailed grant proposal

- A nomination from a specific source named by the award sponsor

- An application

- An application fee

Get an Extra Letter   If an application calls for letters of recommendation, consider getting one more letter than requested in case one of your letter writers is unable to come through.

Get Professional Help   The Grantsmanship Center (TGC) conducts training programs and proposal writing workshops throughout the country. It also produces its own publications and newsletter. Its inexpensive guide ($4.00), "Program Planning and Proposal Writing," offers step-by-step grant writing instructions. For information, write or call:

continues

The Grantsmanship Center
1125 West Sixth Street
P.O. Box 17220
Los Angeles, CA 90017
(213) 482-9860; (800) 421-9512

APPLICATION STRATEGIES

There is much competition for getting outright awards, so be as careful and conscientious in preparing your award application(s) as you are in preparing your admission application. Be sure to:

- Fill out all material as neatly as possible

- Type all applications

- Answer every question

- Answer all questions directly without digressing

- Have someone else read the application for accuracy

When writing essays, personal statements, and proposals:

- Use a computer to prepare your work

- Use a spell- and grammar-checker to proof your work (and be sure to proof it again yourself)

- Print out your work on the best printer available

 Adhere to Deadlines All of the items requested, including transcripts, test scores, and letters of recommendation, must be submitted on time.

WRITING STYLE AND ORGANIZATION

Whether you're writing short or lengthy pieces, you want to be certain your writing meets the highest possible standards. As you evaluate an application, ask yourself the following questions:

- Is your writing objectively written and well thought-out?

- Do you market your ideas accurately? Always recheck facts and figures and obtain the most up-to-date information possible.

- Do you include concrete examples to back up all your ideas?

- Does your writing have coherent organization that leads to a logical conclusion?

- Have you written to the tone of the audience?

- Have you adhered to the specified page limit or word count?

BASIC PROPOSAL STRUCTURE

If you're writing a large proposal, adhere to standard proposal writing guidelines and the requirements of the organization you're applying to. There are formal proposal writing formats that you should adapt as necessary. The following generic outline applies to most proposals:

- **Proposal Summary or Abstract**. Provides a clear and succinct description of your goals.

- **Introduction**. States the purpose of your proposal and defines the scope of your work.

- **Problem Statement**. Defines the problems your work will address.

- **Goals and Objectives**. Shows what you hope to achieve.

- **Methods**. Describes how you will accomplish your goals and objectives.

- **Evaluation**. Demonstrates how you will evaluate your work.

- **Future Funding**. Explains how you will continue your work when the outright award runs out.

- **Budget**. Should be a carefully itemized explanation of your total expenses.

- **Appendix**. Contains any additional supporting material.

FOR FURTHER INFORMATION...

The following books provide helpful information about writing personal statements and essays, and guidance on writing skills in general:

- *The 10 Minute Guide to Applying to Grad School*, by Sharon McDonnell and Ellen Lichtenstein, Alpha Books, 1997, $10.95.

- *Graduate Essays—What Works, What Doesn't, and Why*, by Donald Asher, Ten Speed Press, 1991, $11.95.

- *Webster's New World Student Writing Handbook*, by Sharon Sorenson, Prentice Hall, 1992, $16.00.

- *The Elements of Technical Writing,* by Robert W. Bly and Gary Blake, Macmillan, 1993, $18.00.

 Online Help   Online help for preparing grants is available through the Internet. Indiana University's RUGS site offers extensive grant writing assistance. Its location is http://www.indiana.edu.

SUMMARY

In this lesson, you learned how to write outstanding grant applications and proposals.

12

RESEARCHING SPECIAL FUNDING OPPORTUNITIES

In this lesson, you will learn how to seek out financial aid allocated for special student groups and populations—minorities, women, veterans, international students, and others.

SPECIAL FUNDING OPPORTUNITIES

Targeted aid geared to specific student populations can include grants, fellowships, scholarships, work-study, and loans. This aid is available from government, institutional, and private sources. Targeted aid can be need-based, merit-based, or a combination of the two.

RESEARCHING THE OPPORTUNITIES

There are many resources available for research. They include the following:

- Your school's financial aid office and graduate school admission office

- Your school or local library

- The annual grant directories and online resources listed in lessons 10 and 11

- The U.S. government's excellent handbook, *Higher Education Opportunities for Minorities and Women— Annotated Selections*. It provides thorough educational and financial aid advice for women, minorities, and other groups. For ordering information, write or call: U.S. Government Printing Office, Superintendent of Documents, Washington, D.C. 20402, (202) 512-1800

OPPORTUNITIES FOR WOMEN AND MINORITIES

The following directories are helpful resources for women and minorities:

- *Directory of Financial Aids for Women*, by Gail A. Schlachter and R. David Weber, Reference Service Press, 1994, $45.00

- *Directory of Financial Aids for Minorities*, by Gail A. Schlachter and R. David Weber, Reference Service Press, 1993, $47.50

- *Directory of Special Programs for Minority Group Members*, by Willis L. Johnson, Garret Park Press, 1990, $30.00

Using Online Services   The Minority Online Information Service is a free service providing educational information for minorities. Search for Federal Information Exchange, Inc. (FIE) online, or contact:

continues

Federal Information Exchange, Inc. (FIE)
555 Quince Orchard Road
Gaithersburg, MD 20878
(301) 975-0103
Fax: (301) 975-0109

PROGRAMS TO CONSIDER

The following fellowship programs are considered excellent
and prestigious sources of graduate student support for women
and minorities:

> Ford Foundation Doctoral Fellowships for Minorities
> Fellowship Office
> National Research Council
> 2101 Constitution Avenue
> Washington, D.C. 20418
> (202) 334-2872
> Deadline: early November

> National Consortium for Graduate Degrees for Minorities
> in Engineering and Science (GEM)
> P.O. Box 537
> Notre Dame, IN 46556
> (219) 287-1097
> Deadline: December 1

> National Physical Science Consortium
> (minorities and women in selected fields)
> Student Recruitment Office
> New Mexico State University
> P.O. Box 30001, Dept. 3NPS
> Las Cruces, NM 88003-8001
> (505) 646-6038
> Deadline: November 15

National Science Foundation Fellowships
(minority and non-minority competition)
Oak Ridge Associated Universities
P.O. Box 3010
Oak Ridge, TN 37831-3010
(615) 241-4300
Deadline: early November

Patricia Roberts Harris Fellowships
(for women and minorities)
Office of Postsecondary Education
U.S. Department of Education
400 Maryland Avenue, SW
Washington, D.C. 20202
(202) 708-7127
Deadline: deadlines vary by institutions

Using Computerized Search Services   Computer search services exist that match students with appropriate school and graduate programs. Specifically, the GRE Student Locator Service, which matches students with schools, can prove extremely useful to minority students. The service is free for prospective graduate school applicants, and GRE registration is not required. For more information, contact:

Graduate Record Examination (GRE)
Student Search Service
P.O. Box 6000
Princeton, NJ 08541-6000
(609) 771-7670

OPPORTUNITIES FOR VETERANS

There are several federal benefits programs providing financial assistance to veterans, disabled veterans, and dependents of deceased or disabled veterans. Veterans should contact their Veterans Administration regional office to get free information about educational benefits available. They can get toll-free service by calling (800) 827-1000.

Veterans can also order *Federal Benefits for Veterans and Dependents* from the government. The cost is $2.50. Contact:

> Superintendent of Documents
> U.S. Government Printing Office
> Washington, D.C. 20402

Another useful resource is *Financial Aid for Veterans, Military Personnel, and Their Dependents*, by Gail A. Schlachter and R. David Weber, the Reference Service Press, 1994, $38.50.

For further help, veterans should check with their school financial aid office and state financial aid office. Individual states may also offer veterans assistance programs.

OPPORTUNITIES FOR STUDENTS STUDYING OVERSEAS

Students who want to study overseas should obtain a copy of *Study Abroad*, published by the United Nations Educational, Scientific and Cultural Organization (UNESCO). Cost is $24. For ordering information, write to Unipub, Inc., 4611-F Assembly Drive, Lanham, MD 20706.

Work, Study, Travel Abroad: The Whole World Handbook, from the Council on International Educational Exchange (CIEE), provides sound advice on graduate study. The cost is $12.95. For ordering information, contact the CIEE, Publications Department, 205 East 42nd Street, New York, NY 10017.

OPPORTUNITIES FOR DISABLED STUDENTS

Disabled students should see if their library has the following publications:

* *Financial Aid for the Disabled and Their Families*, by Gail A. Schlachter and R. David Weber, Reference Service Press, 1994, $38.50

* *Directory of Grants for Organizations Serving People with Disabilities*, by Richard Echstein, Research Grant Guides, 1993, $49.50

The Pocket Guide to Federal Help for Individuals with Disabilities can be ordered from the Government Printing Office. Cost is $1.50. For information, write to Superintendent of Documents, U.S. Government Printing Office, Washington, D.C. 20402.

OPPORTUNITIES FOR FOREIGN STUDENTS

While much of the federal and state aid discussed in this book is not available to foreign students, private and institutional support is available, especially in the form of teaching and research assistantships. Foreign students may also have restrictions on the work opportunities available to them because of Immigration and Naturalization Service (INS) requirements.

Foreign students have to know the policies of the schools they want to attend, because some institutions may not admit foreign students who are not totally self-supporting. Foreign students should begin their research early and seek advice from their own government, the U.S. embassy, and the Fulbright commission office in their country.

For more information, see *Funding for U.S. Study: A Guide for Foreign Nationals*. You can obtain this from the Institute of International Education, 809 United Nations Plaza, New York, NY 10017-3580.

SUMMARY

In this lesson, you learned about targeted funding for women and minorities, veterans, students studying overseas, disabled students, and foreign students.

13

ESTIMATING YOUR FINANCIAL STANDING

In this lesson, you will learn how to determine your net worth to estimate how much money you have to pay for graduate school.

CALCULATING YOUR NET WORTH

Assuming you have decided to go to graduate school, you have to realistically assess your current financial worth. Your *contribution*—how much you can afford to pay—plays a large factor in how much aid you will receive.

One way to estimate your contribution is to calculate your net worth. Your net worth is determined by subtracting your liabilities from your assets.

ADDING UP YOUR ASSETS

For financial planning, *assets* are usually divided into several categories: liquid (cash or easily converted into cash); investment (assets intended to increase in value for future needs); and personal (items for your own use). These categories are further explained in the following list:

- **Liquid Assets**. Examples of liquid assets include cash, cash equivalents, and short-term investments such as savings accounts, money market funds, certificates of deposit, cash value of life insurance, and short-term Treasury Bills.

- **Investment Assets**. Examples include stocks, bonds, real estate, and Individual Retirement Accounts (IRAs).

- **Personal Assets**. Examples include your home or personal residence, car, and collectibles (such as stamps and coins).

ADDING UP YOUR LIABILITIES

Liabilities are your debts—the money you owe against assets. For example, credit card debt and loans are liabilities. Financial planning usually classifies liabilities as short- or long-term obligations. The following list further explains these two types of liabilities:

- **Short-Term Obligations**. Liabilities that must be paid off within one year, including amounts on long-term obligations that must be paid within that time. Examples include credit card payments and installment loans.

- **Long-Term Obligations**. Liabilities used to finance major personal assets or long-term investments. Examples include residential mortgages and college loans.

GETTING YOUR FIGURES ON PAPER

Your first step is to get your net worth on paper. Only by seeing figures in black and white can you have a clear picture of your financial situation.

Take the time to do this accurately. Get all your financial records together as though you were doing your income tax return. This is an important strategy that will pay off later when you have to provide similar information on financial aid application forms.

First, calculate your assets:

A. Liquid Assets

Cash   _____

Short-term investments   _____

Life insurance cash value   _____

Total   _____

B. Investment Assets

Stocks   _____

Bonds   _____

Mutual funds   _____

Retirement accounts   _____

Other   _____

Total   _____

C. Personal Assets

Personal residence   _____

Vacation residence   _____

Automobile   _____

Collectibles   _____

Other   _____

Total   _____

D. Total Assets   _____

Now, calculate how much money you owe:

A. Short-Term Obligations

Credit card debt   _____

Installment loans   _____

Personal loans   _____

Life insurance
borrowings   _____

Accrued income taxes   _____

Total   _____

B. Long-Term Obligations

School loans (long-term) _____

Personal residences
mortgages   _____

Loans to finance
investments   _____

Other   _____

Total   _____

C. Total Liabilities _____

Finally, find your net worth by subtracting your liabilities from your assets:

Total Assets _____

– Total Liabilities _____

= Net Worth _____

ESTIMATING HOW MUCH MORE MONEY YOU NEED

After you calculate your net worth, you should have a good idea of how much money you have available to fund your graduate school education. Most likely, you will not have enough to pay for your education.

By comparing your financial standing to the total costs of attendance you calculated in Lesson 3, you can begin to assess the remaining amount you will need.

SUMMARY

In this lesson, you learned how to assess your net worth and determine how much more money you will need to pay for graduate school.

14

PREPARING A SAVINGS PLAN

In this lesson, you will learn how to estimate your savings needs and evaluate savings plans.

SAVING FOR YOUR GRADUATE EDUCATION

You can bridge the gap between what graduate school will cost you and what you can afford to pay by implementing an aggressive savings plan.

While your parents and grandparents may have helped pay for your undergraduate education, odds are you will be in charge of saving for your graduate education. And your time horizon—the number of years you have to save—will be a lot shorter. Assume you have a time horizon of five years or less.

To get a handle on your savings needs, prepare savings worksheets for your two or three top graduate school choices. Use the estimated cost of attendance figures you calculated from Lesson 3 and remember to use a seven percent inflation factor for each year of your graduate school education. Use the following table as a model to prepare your worksheets.

SAVINGS TARGET WORKSHEET

School Name   Years in School   Dollars Needed

_____   _____   _____

total costs   _____

less amount now saved   _____

savings target   _____

SAVING SHORT TERM

As you choose among savings and investment plans, you should look for the safest possible vehicles that give you the best interest rates. Safety of principle should be your greatest concern. With a time horizon of less than five years, you should choose from the following methods, which are the safest savings and investment vehicles available:

- **Passbook Savings Accounts through Banks, Credit Unions, or Savings and Loans.** These are the most basic types of savings plans and the ones that will yield the lowest interest. You can usually open a savings account with a small sum. Passbook savings are Federal Deposit Insurance Corporation (FDIC) insured.

- **Money-Market Deposit Accounts (MMDAs) and Money Market Mutual Funds.** Both vehicles should give you a percentage point or more of interest above passbook savings. MMDAs are FDIC insured; money market mutual funds are not.

- **Certificates of Deposit (CDs).** CDs yield higher interest rates than passbook savings and MMDAs.

However, CDs require that you tie up a minimum amount of money for a certain period of time—anywhere from three months to five years. Bank CDs are FDIC insured.

- **Savings Bonds through Banks or Employee Deduction.** Backed by the federal government, these will pay you a guaranteed interest rate if you hold them for five years.

- **Treasury Bills and Notes.** Backed by the federal government, both of these types of securities will pay you high interest. The minimum amount required for purchasing short-term bills (with terms of one year or less) is $10,000; notes (with terms of less than four years) are sold at a minimum of $5,000; and notes (with terms four years and over) are sold at a minimum of $1,000.

- **Short- to Medium-Term Bond Mutual Funds.** While these options involve taking on more risk than the previous vehicles, they are appropriate investments. Use short-term funds if your time horizon is less than two years.

Researching Your Savings and Investment Options

There are many excellent books and magazines about personal finance that can help you. If you want to seek the advice of a financial professional, read up and know the basics before asking for advice. The following paperbacks are excellent introductions to personal finance:

- *Complete Idiot's Guide to Managing Your Money,* by Robert K. Heady and Christy Heady, Alpha Books, 1995, $16.99. Offers sound advice on savings, investments, and debt management.

- *Your First Financial Steps* by Nancy Dunnan, Harper Perennial, 1995, $12.00. Top-notch guide for the recent college graduate or financial novice that includes helpful strategies on paying down student debt.

 Use Payroll Deduction or Automatic Investment Plans If you work, both of these plans allow for a disciplined approach to savings. If you have money taken out of your paycheck before you get it, or have money electronically transferred from your bank account each month, you will miss the money less.

SPECIAL COLLEGE SAVINGS PLANS

Over the past few years, private companies have been marketing college savings plans. Some of these vehicles can be used for graduate school. One such plan is the CollegeSure CD from the College Savings Bank. The interest rate on the CD is recalculated annually based on the rate of college inflation. For more information, write or call:

College Savings Bank
5 Vaughn Drive
Princeton, NJ 08540-6313
(800) 888-2723

SUMMARY

In this lesson, you learned how to estimate your savings goal and choose an appropriate savings plan.

15

BEGINNING THE FINANCIAL AID APPLICATION PROCESS

In this lesson, you will learn how to begin to apply for financial aid.

OVERVIEW OF THE APPLICATION PROCESS

Figure 15.1 gives you an overview of the financial aid application process. While this process can be intimidating to many students, over the next few lessons you will learn a systematic plan of approach that will make the process easier.

TAKING THE FIRST STEP

Your first step in finding and applying for financial aid is to contact the financial aid office at each school you're interested in for information and applications. Do this as soon as possible.

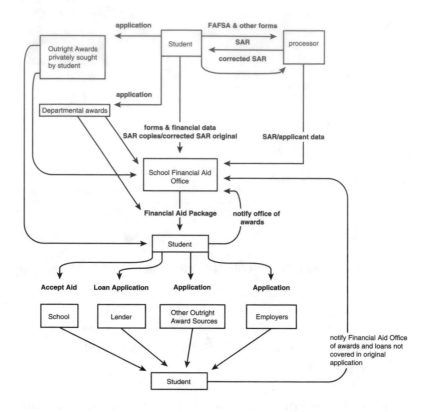

Figure 15.1   Overview of the financial aid application process.

A financial aid administrator will discuss the financial aid process with you and will provide you with all of the forms the school requires. He or she is also the best source of information about alternate aid sources that the school doesn't provide.

FINDING OTHER SOURCES OF AID

At the same time you are applying to schools, you should start seeking out sources of outright awards (which do not have to be repaid), as well as exploring work opportunities such as assistantships. Get started as soon as possible. The deadlines for many outright awards often fall far in advance of school admission and financial aid applications.

 Exploring Department Assistance Many graduate school departments give out highly valued awards based on departmental and faculty recommendations. When you apply to graduate programs, you should schedule interviews with faculty and potential advisors. You should also find out from the graduate school admission office and individual departments what assistance is available.

GETTING THE RIGHT APPLICATIONS

First, get copies of all the forms you will need, both for individual schools and for other forms of aid. Make sure you have the most current version of each form. The forms you need can include the following:

- Free Application for Federal Student Aid (FAFSA) form

- Financial Aid PROFILE from the College Scholarship Service—this has supplanted the Financial Aid Form (FAF)

- School applications

- Departmental applications

- State financial aid applications

- Individual loan applications

- Applications from all outright award funding sources

You can get many of the forms from the school financial aid office. Read Lesson 16 to find out how filling out application forms correctly is critical in getting financial aid.

Get Multiple Copies and Keep Records   Get several copies of all applications. Read them and be sure to ask questions if you don't understand any of the requirements. Don't be shy about calling any financial aid office—school, state, and federal— to answer your questions. Keep copies of your completed forms.

MANAGING THE APPLICATION PROCESS

As a financial aid applicant, you must manage the financial aid application process. While financial aid offices are sometimes hectic places, the administrators will do their best to answer your questions. You have the right to ask the following questions of the school:

- What is the availability of financial aid on all federal, state, local, private, and institutional programs?

- How does the school select financial aid recipients?

- What are the procedures and deadlines for submitting applications for each financial aid program?

- How will the school determine my financial need?

- How are costs of attendance calculated (including tuition and fees, room and board, travel, books and supplies, and personal and miscellaneous expenses)?

- What resources are assessed to calculate my financial need (for example, student contribution, other sources of financial aid, and other assets)?

- How does the school determine the distribution of awards and award amounts in the financial aid package?

- What is the process for reassessing my aid package if a mistake is made or if my enrollment or financial circumstances change?

- How and when will I receive my aid?

- Which aid, if any, is contingent upon my making satisfactory academic progress? How does the school define satisfactory academic progress? What happens if my academic performance is unsatisfactory?

- What are the interest rates on my student loan(s)? How much time do I have to repay the loan(s)? When must I start repayment? What cancellation, discharge, forbearance, or deferment provisions apply to my loan(s)?

- For students with federal work-study jobs: What is my job? What are my hours, duties, and rate of pay? How and when will I be paid?

- What are the location, hours, and counseling procedures of the financial aid office?

Communicating with Schools It is your job to manage the financial aid application process. As the manager, you must promptly respond to all mail sent regarding financial aid. Read all letters immediately and do whatever is requested of you.

SUMMARY

In this lesson, you received an overview of the financial aid application process, including how to receive applications, which applications you may need, and the information you have a right to request from the financial aid office.

16

FILING AND PROCESSING APPLICATION FORMS

In this lesson, you will learn how to fill out financial aid applications correctly, including the Free Application for Federal Student Aid (FAFSA) form.

THE FAFSA

Understanding the FAFSA form is important. You fill it out when applying for federal aid as well as for much state and institutional funding. In fact, many schools use the FAFSA as their only application form in the financial aid process.

FEDERAL AID THROUGH THE FAFSA FORM

For graduate students, the FAFSA application covers several programs:

- Federal Perkins Loans
- Subsidized Stafford Loans
- Unsubsidized Stafford Loans
- Federal Work-Study (FWS)

Check Other Forms   Always make sure you ask about and complete all forms necessary for your loan. For example, in addition to the FAFSA, Stafford Loan applicants must also complete the Federal Stafford Loan Application and Promissory Note.

INFORMATION REQUESTED ON THE FAFSA

The FAFSA requests basic educational and financial information, which is summarized in the following list:

- **Basic Information.** Your name, address, social security number, and so on.

- **Educational Background.** The educational level completed by you and by your parents.

- **Educational Plans.** Your course of study, the degree you expect to attain, the financial aid you're interested in, and so on.

- **Student Status.** Your marital status, the number of dependents you have, and so on.

- **Household Information.** Information on the number of people in your household.

- **Income, Earnings, and Benefits.** Your income and tax information (and your spouse's, if applicable).

- **Asset Information.** Sources and amounts of your assets (and your spouse's, if applicable).

- **Releases and Signatures.** Names of the colleges to which you want your FAFSA sent.

Use the following list as a checklist as you compile the information and records needed to complete the FAFSA and other financial aid applications:

- Tax returns for the previous year (federal, state, and local returns) or previous year's estimated returns
- Parents' tax returns, if required
- All W-2 statements for the previous year (or other records of earnings and taxable income, such as 1099 forms)
- Current bank statements
- Current mortgage information
- Business and farm records
- Documentation of non-taxable income (such as social security or veterans benefits)
- Stocks, bonds, and other investment statements showing interest dividends and capital gains received
- Social security number
- Driver's license

Take Time to Fill Out the FAFSA   The FAFSA is probably the most difficult of the financial aid forms you will have to fill out. If you do it accurately and have all your records in order, completing other forms will seem easy in comparison. While the government estimates that it takes approximately one to one-and-a-half hours to fill out the FAFSA, you may find that your FAFSA application takes a lot longer.

First do a dry run. Make a copy of the FAFSA and fill it out in pencil. Review it. Then fill out the version you will send in.

 Get FAFSA Assistance   You can contact the Federal Student Aid Information Center, 9 a.m. to 8 p.m. eastern standard time, Monday through Friday, at (800) 433-3243, or (800) 730-8913 for the hearing impaired.

If you are a working professional, self-employed, or have financial assets, you should consider asking your accountant or financial planner to help you with the FAFSA.

The following guide takes you through the FAFSA step by step and is appropriate for both graduate and undergraduate students:

> *College Financial Aid Made Easy*, by Patrick L. Bellantoni, Tara Publishing, 1995, $24.95. Written by a Certified Financial Planner, this excellent resource provides detailed tax and financial information.

 Check on Electronic FAFSA Processing Certain schools can process the FAFSA electronically. Check with your school financial aid administrator to see if this is a possibility. It will speed up the application process.

THE STUDENT AID REPORT (SAR)

After completing the FAFSA, you will send it in to either the processor listed on the form or to the school, if the school files

the FAFSA itself. (If a school files the FAFSA from its own offices, it will tell you so in its application information.)

Applying to Several Schools   Don't worry about
filing separate FAFSA forms. You can only file one
FAFSA each year. On the FAFSA, you can list up
to six schools that can receive your processed
financial data—called the Student Aid Report
(SAR). If you want additional schools to receive the
SAR, you should call the financial aid administrators at those schools and ask them how to do this.

If you file by mail, your application will be processed in approximately four weeks. You will then receive a Student Aid
Report (SAR) in the mail. The SAR restates the information you
entered on the FAFSA and gives you a calculated EFC—the
amount you will be expected to contribute. The schools you
designated on the FAFSA also receive a copy of the SAR.

Expected Family Contribution (EFC)   For
graduate students, this is the amount that you and
your spouse are expected to contribute to your
educational costs.

If you file the FAFSA electronically, your application will be
processed in about a week. The results will be sent to your
school and you will also receive a copy of the SAR in the mail.

READING AND CORRECTING THE SAR

Reading, verifying, and correcting the SAR is essential. When
you receive the SAR, follow these steps:

1. If you have to make changes, make them in Part 2 of the SAR and return it to the address given at the end of Part 2. (To be safe, send your changes via certified mail, return receipt requested.) After a few weeks, you will receive a revised SAR to check.

2. If you have special circumstances you need to bring to the attention of the financial aid administrator, see the section "Special Circumstances," later in this lesson.

3. If the school is doing the filing, you will have to sign the SAR Certification Statement at the financial aid office. If the SAR requires changes, check with the financial aid administrator on how to handle it.

4. If the data is correct and you don't need to make changes, you will then receive financial aid on the basis of that information.

5. Keep several copies of the SAR for yourself. You can also request a duplicate SAR by writing to the address listed on the SAR.

6. The original SAR should only be sent to the school you will attend. Always send the original via certified mail, return receipt requested.

SAR Assistance   If you have not received your SAR four weeks after you filed the FAFSA, you can check on the application by calling (319) 337-5665 (Monday through Friday, 9 a.m. to 8 p.m., eastern standard time). Or write to: Federal Student Information Aid Center, P.O. Box 84, Washington, D.C. 20044.

tip **Saving Time** If you are certain about the school you want to attend and have made changes to the SAR, ask a financial aid administrator at the school if you should send the corrected original copy.

SPECIAL CIRCUMSTANCES

Although the process of determining a student's eligibility for aid is basically the same for all applicants, there is some flexibility. For example, if you can document a special circumstance that affects your need for financial aid, your financial aid administrator can adjust your cost of attendance (budget) or income information used to calculate your expected family (student) contribution.

Special circumstances can include:

- High medical and dental expenses for you or your spouse
- Divorce or separation
- Your or your spouse's unemployment
- Death or disability of spouse

This is not an inclusive list. It's up to you to tell the financial aid administrator what circumstances affect you. The financial aid administrator will use professional judgment in deciding your case.

Handling Special Circumstances   It's best to deal with special circumstances when you correct the SAR. You should send a copy of the corrected SAR with a letter to the financial aid administrator, who will contact you after reviewing your request. You must be prepared to document your special circumstances according to the financial aid administrator's directions. All decisions from the financial aid administrator are final and cannot be appealed to the U.S. Department of Education.

FINANCIAL AID PROFILE

This needs-analysis form written and processed by the College Scholarship Service (CSS) has replaced the Financial Aid Form (FAF). Many graduate schools use the PROFILE as well as their own forms to determine your eligibility for institutional aid.

The financial aid administrator will tell you how to register for the PROFILE. Be certain to fill out the form carefully. In some cases, a school will ask for information on the PROFILE not requested on the FAFSA (such as parental information). After submitting the PROFILE, you will receive an acknowledgment letter from CSS approximately two weeks later. Like the SAR, you should check this for accuracy. The letter will tell you how to submit necessary corrections.

SUMMARY

In this lesson, you learned how to fill out the FAFSA and the PROFILE and how to handle the Student Aid Report.

MANAGING DEADLINES

In this lesson, you will learn how to use deadlines to your advantage as part of your funding strategy.

BEATING DEADLINES

Knowing and beating deadlines is extremely important when you apply for admission and financial aid. You must meet deadlines involving the following:

- Standardized testing
- School applications and admission
- Financial aid from all sources you seek out
- Departmental requirements

The following sections explain these deadlines in more detail.

TESTING DEADLINES

For each of the following tests, you must meet different registration and score submission deadlines.

- Graduate Record Examination (GRE) General Test
- GRE Subject Test(s)
- Miller Analogies Test (MAT)
- Test of English as a Foreign Language (TOEFL) (if necessary for international students)

ADMISSION DEADLINES

For each school you are interested in, you must submit complete and neatly prepared applications with all requirements including:

- Application fees
- Official academic and financial transcripts
- Personal statements and essays
- Letters of recommendation
- Work samples
- Address labels

FINANCIAL AID DEADLINES

You must submit all required forms and proposals to all parties (including school, federal, state, and private processors) as required.

PREPARING A DEADLINE CALENDAR

As early as possible, prepare a calendar of all critical dates you must meet (check that you have the correct dates). To do this, either use a yearly calendar you can write on or prepare a generic monthly worksheet.

Be aggressive. Review each month's worksheet the month before to ensure that you're getting your applications ready and doing the necessary work to meet your schedule.

TESTING DEADLINES

Many schools prefer you take the October GRE for very practical reasons. It takes six weeks for the scores to be reported to the school after testing. Because many schools have January application cutoffs, tests taken after October will probably arrive too late. This will delay your admission decisions and seriously affect any decisions about financial aid awards.

Schedule and start preparing for all tests you're required to take as early as possible. Get the testing schedules and application forms from the agencies in the following list. Find out the policy on retaking tests if you are unhappy with your scores.

> Graduate Record Examinations (GRE)
> Educational Testing Service
> P.O. Box 6000
> Princeton, NJ 08541-6014
> (609) 771-7690

> Miller Analogies Test (MAT)
> 555 Academic Court
> San Antonio, TX 78204-3956
> (210) 921-8801 or (800) 622-3231

> Test of English as a Foreign Language (TOEFL)
> P.O. Box 6151
> Princeton, NJ 08541-6151
> (609) 921-9000

Exam Preparation   Plan on studying for your tests at least three months before taking them. If you're taking several exams, you may want to take them on different test dates. If you have been out of school for several years, you should seriously consider enrolling in an exam preparation course.

ADMISSION DEADLINES

You should aim to get your admission applications in at least a month before the required deadline. Set up your deadline worksheet so that all application components (letters of recommendation, transcripts, and so on) from outside sources are mailed to you several months before the deadline date. Photocopy your application and all documentation before mailing them to the school. If you wait until the last minute to send your application in, mail it via registered mail.

Check on Your Application   Call each school you have applied to several days before the deadline to make sure your package has been received.

FINANCIAL AID DEADLINES

Remember, financial aid deadlines do not necessarily coincide with admission deadlines; in many cases, they come earlier.

A school cannot award you any financial aid unless you have been accepted for admission.

STATE AID

Each state has different financial aid deadlines. If you're applying to schools in different states, make sure you have the right deadline information.

Check the FAFSA Deadlines for state student aid are listed on the Free Application for Federal Student Aid (FAFSA).

OUTRIGHT AWARDS

Many of the most prestigious grants, fellowships, and scholarships have very early deadlines—in October and November. If you're unable to apply for them for your first year of graduate school, aim to apply for your next.

The Earlier the Better For many types of aid, such as outright awards, state aid, and the campus-based Perkins Loan and Federal Work-Study programs, your chances of getting aid depend on the availability of funding. Therefore, the earlier you apply, the better. However, remember not to apply earlier than stipulated—federal student aid applications cannot be submitted before January 1.

CAMPUS-BASED PROGRAMS

Each school sets its own deadlines for students applying to the federal Perkins Loan and Federal Work-Study (FWS) programs.

The deadlines may be the same as the school's own financial aid deadline. In any case, the deadlines will usually be earlier than the U.S. Department of Education's spring deadline. Be sure to get the right deadline information.

 Deadlines and Taxes   Don't miss any deadlines because you haven't completed your income tax returns for the base year. Have a professional tax preparer prepare estimated tax returns for you to use. Keep all your payroll stubs; your last payroll stub for the year will be a good record of your earnings if you have not yet received your W-2 forms.

Finally, remember, even if you miss your school or state financial aid deadlines, you probably can meet the deadline for federal financial aid (non-campus-based), which falls in the spring.

SUMMARY

In this lesson, you learned about how to meet testing, admission, and financial aid deadlines.

Understanding the Financial Award Package

In this lesson, you will learn about financial aid packages and how they are awarded.

Getting the Package

If the school's financial aid office determines that you're eligible for aid, you will receive a financial award letter announcing your financial aid award package. You will also be notified if you are denied aid. However, you will only receive an award letter after:

- You have been accepted for admission.
- You have met all the financial aid application requirements.

In some instances, your award letter will arrive in the same envelope as your graduate school acceptance letter.

Packages are put together by the financial aid office on the basis of the following:

- Your completed application, including all requested supporting documents

- Your enrollment status—full- or part-time

- The availability of federal, state, and institutional funds

UNDERSTANDING THE AWARD LETTER

Be sure to read the award letter carefully. Each school has its own letter format, and some schools provide more detail than others. Elements to look for in a letter include:

- Listing of each type of aid awarded by the school

- Dollar amount of each award

- Time period covered by the award

- Listing of awards, such as grants and fellowships, you have already received from other sources

- Formula showing how the award was determined— the estimated total cost of your attendance (budget)

- Your Expected Family Contribution (EFC)

- Your financial aid eligibility

- Total award value

- Unmet need—that part of the package for which you're eligible but the college is unable to fund

All award letters should document the first three items in the list. Take a look at the following sample student award letter.

OFFICE OF STUDENT FINANCIAL ASSISTANCE

April 15, 1997

Ms. Sandy Jones
100 Main Street
Indianapolis, IN 46204

Dear Ms. Jones:

We are very pleased to award you the following financial aid for the 1997-1998 academic year.

Please read this letter carefully. You must return one signed copy of this letter to us by May 15, 1997 or risk cancellation of your award.

Indicate your acceptance of each type of aid listed below by checking the appropriate space provided.

Type of Aid	1997 Fall	1998 Spring	Total	Accept	Reject
Merit Scholarship	$2,500	$2,500	$5,000	_____	_____
Federal Stafford Loan	$3,000	$3,000	$6,000	_____	_____
Federal Perkins Loan	$2,000	$2,000	$4,000	_____	_____
Federal Work-Study	$1,500	$1,500	$3,000	_____	_____
Totals Awarded	$9,000	$9,000	$18,000	_____	_____

Your award was determined from your signifying full-time status for the periods indicated and according to the following costs:

Costs of Attendance:	$23,000
Less Student Contribution:	−3,000
Financial Aid Eligibility:	$20,000
Total Award Package:	$18,000
Unmet Need:	$2,000

Please sign, date, and return one copy of this letter to indicate your acceptance or rejection of this package. Please call the Financial Aid Office if you have any questions.

Accepted:

Signature:_____ Date:_____

Rejected:

Signature:_____ Date:_____

CHOOSING THE BEST AWARD PACKAGE

Review each award letter you receive. Be sure to call the financial aid office if you are unsure when or how you will receive any awards. As you decide among award packages, you should consider all factors including:

- Which college will cost the least overall

- The different terms for all loans awarded

- Which school offers the most outright awards (awards that don't have to be repaid)

- The terms of any scholarships or assistantships included in the award

- Which school will, in your opinion, provide the best education

SETTING UP A COMPARISON CHART

To make your task easier, set up an award comparison chart for the schools you want to attend. Use the following as your model. It was adapted with permission from the New England Education Loan Marketing Association (Nellie Mae).

1. List the total cost of each school. You can get this information from your award letter. If the data is not in the letter, call the financial aid office.

	School 1	School 2	School 3
	_____	_____	_____
	Name	Name	Name
Cost of Attendance	$_____	$_____	$_____

2. List the financial aid awards being offered from each
   school. What portion of each financial aid package is
   made up of grants, scholarships, fellowships, work,
   and loans?

Outright Awards—Fellowships, Grants, and Scholar-ships

	School 1	School 2	School 3
	Name	Name	Name
School Awards			
State Awards			
Federal Awards			
Other			
A. Total	$	$	$

Work Opportunities

Federal Work Study			
Assistantships			
Other			
B. Total	$	$	$

Loans

Subsidized Stafford			
Unsubsidized Stafford			
Perkins			
Other			
Other			
C. Total	$	$	$
Total Aid (A+B+C)	$	$	$

3. List the amount (unmet need) that the school has determined you will be expected to pay toward your school costs beyond what is offered in the letter.

School 1   School 2   School 3

_____   _____   _____

Name   Name   Name

$ _____ $ _____ $ _____

4. Combine this information with your educational and personal expectations to choose the school that is best for you. Remember that your financial aid award in your second year will not necessarily be the same as the one awarded in your first year.

ASSESSING LOANS AS A FACTOR IN THE AWARD PACKAGE

Look carefully at the amount of loans included in the financial aid package. Because loans have to be repaid, add the total amount of loans to the amount of money you have to come up with.

For example, if a $20,000 financial aid package consisted of $10,000 in outright awards and $10,000 in loans, you should add that $10,000 to the total you need to come up with.

ASSESSING OTHER COST FACTORS

At this time, you should re-estimate the budget you prepared in Lesson 3 to see if you can cut expenses. While you should cut all non-essential expenses, you should also ask yourself if the cost of attendance is reasonable. Does the budget reasonably allow for necessities?

If it will be necessary to draw on assets you didn't anticipate using, carefully consider the consequences before doing so.

NEGOTIATING A BETTER PACKAGE

You may be provided with instructions in the letter on how to appeal data with which you disagree. Although there is probably little you can do at this time to change the basic terms offered, you may be able to request certain changes (such as increasing work-study while reducing a loan). Be certain to put your request in writing and make your request as soon as possible. Appealing an award does not jeopardize the package already awarded.

 Reporting Other Aid If the award package doesn't list other aid you have received, such as assistantships or private scholarships, notify the financial aid office immediately. Certain types of aid will not affect your financial aid eligibility, but others will.

ACCEPTING THE AWARD PACKAGE

If you're accepting the package, sign and return the letter by the indicated date. Don't miss the return deadline. Be sure to keep your copy of the award letter in an individual file set up to store your financial aid information.

Funding Unmet Need   Unmet need can be met with such financial aid as assistantships, grants, and loans. Each is discussed in separate lessons in this book. Remember—while it may be too late to seek outright awards for the coming year, you should always think ahead and plan for the next academic year.

SUMMARY

In this lesson, you learned how to compare financial aid award packages and finalize the financial aid process.

19

UNDERSTANDING FEDERAL LOAN REPAYMENT

In this lesson, you will learn borrower rights and responsibilities and the conditions under which you can defer—or even cancel— loan repayment.

UNDERSTANDING YOUR RESPONSIBILITIES AND RIGHTS

As a borrower, you have certain responsibilities and rights which must be understood before you take on debt. Never, under any condition, borrow money without understanding the provisions of the loan. This section explains your responsibilities and rights as a loan borrower.

> ***tip*** **Loan Counseling** Regardless of the type of loan you borrow, you must receive entrance counseling before you're given your first loan disbursement, and you must receive exit counseling before you leave school. These counseling sessions will be administered by your school or lender and will
>
> *continues*

provide you with important information about your loan, including the name of the loan representative who manages your loan.

When you sign a promissory note, you agree to do the following (the borrower's responsibilities):

- Repay the loan according to the terms of the note. Except for the conditions listed later in this chapter, you must repay the loan. Going into *default* (failing to repay the loan) can have serious consequences. Your credit rating may be seriously affected, and your lender can ask your employer to deduct payments from your wages.

Default   A borrower's failure to repay a loan according to the terms previously agreed to is called default.

- Make loan repayments even if you don't receive a bill or repayment notice.

- Continue to make payments if you apply for a deferment or forbearance (period of time during which you do not have to make repayments), until you are notified that your request has been granted.

- Notify the lender or lender's representative when you: graduate; withdraw from school; transfer to another school; drop below half-time status; or change your name, address, or social security number.

Before your school makes your first loan disbursement, you will be informed of the following from your school or lender:

- The full amount of the loan

- The interest rate

- When you must begin repayment

- Your eligibility for other types of financial aid

- A complete list of loan fees and how the fees are collected

- The yearly and total amounts you can borrow

- The maximum repayment periods and minimum repayment amount

- An explanation of default and its consequences

- An explanation of consolidating and refinancing options

- A statement of penalty-free prepayment terms

Before you leave school, you will be notified of the following from your school or lender:

- The amount of your total debt, interest rate, and total loan interest charges

- The loan repayment schedule

- The name of the lender or loan service center, the place to send payments, and whom to contact for more information

- Fees for late payments and delinquency or default charges

- A statement of penalty-free prepayment terms

- Current descriptions of your loans, including an estimate of the average total debt and the average monthly payments of students from your school

- A description of applicable deferment, forbearance, and discharge provisions

- Advice about debt management

- Notification about your supplying school with all personal data required

Lesson 5 discussed repayment terms and conditions; however, there are instances when loan deferment, forbearance, or even cancellation may be considered for Perkins and Subsidized and Unsubsidized Stafford Loans.

 Deferment   Postponing a loan repayment is called deferment.

DEFERRING FEDERAL LOANS

Under certain conditions, you can postpone payment on all three types of federal loans. You can apply to the lender for deferment under the following conditions:

- Part-time study at an eligible school

- Study in an approved graduate fellowship or in a rehabilitation training program for the disabled

- Inability to find full-time work, and economic hardship

See the section "Canceling Perkins Loans" later in this lesson for other conditions that qualify you for deferment under the Perkins Loan Program.

UNDERSTANDING FORBEARANCE

All lenders want to get their money back and are usually willing to work out a special arrangement with you if you're willing—but unable—to meet your scheduled repayments.

Forbearance   Refers to an agreement in which a lender and a borrower change the loan repayment schedule.

Forbearance is not unique to the federal student loan program. Forbearance is always subject to the discretion of the lender.

You may request forbearance to allow for any of the following:

- A short period of time during which you make no repayments

- An extension of time for making repayments

- A period of time during which you make smaller payments than were originally scheduled

Because forbearance is discretionary, your lender may ask for a formal written request and other information.

Automatic Forbearance   Loan holders will be required to grant you forbearance when:

- Your annual debt burden for loans under the Federal Family Education Loan (FFEL) Program equals or exceeds 20 percent of your disposable income

- You're serving in a national service position and receiving a national service education award under the National and Community Service Trust Act of 1993

Canceling Loans

In certain instances, you can cancel Perkins or Stafford Loans. The following sections outline these instances.

Canceling Perkins Loans

Several conditions, listed in the following table, qualify the borrower for loan cancellation under the Perkins Loan Program.

Discharge Cancellation Summary for Perkins Loans*

Cancellation Eligibility	Amount Canceled
Special education teacher	up to 100 percent
Teacher for low-income students	up to 100 percent
Professional provider of early intervention services for the disabled	up to 100 percent
Teacher in designated teacher shortage area fields	up to 100 percent
Public or nonprofit family service agency employee serving high-risk, low-income community families	up to 100 percent
Nurse or medical technician	up to 100 percent
Law enforcement or corrections officer	up to 100 percent
Service in a Head Start Program	up to 100 percent
Service as a Vista or Peace Corps volunteer	up to 100 percent
Service in the Armed Forces in area of hostilities or eminent danger	up to 50 percent
Death or disability	100 percent

CANCELLATION ELIGIBILITY	AMOUNT CANCELED
Bankruptcy	amount varies
School closed (before student could complete course of study) or school falsely certified student	0 percent

For all conditions except the last three, the condition also qualifies for deferment.

CANCELING STAFFORD LOANS

Only a few conditions exist for canceling Stafford Loans:

- Borrower's death or permanent disability

- Borrower's bankruptcy

- Borrower's inability to complete a course of study because the institution closed or borrower's eligibility was falsely certified by the institution

DEFAULTING ON LOANS

Always try to work with your lender if you're in financial trouble. Lenders want their money and will work with you to avoid default.

A default will:

- Be reported to national credit bureau organizations

- Adversely affect your credit history

- Possibly make you subject to income-contingent repayment, during which you may lose assets and/or be subject to wage garnishment (a percentage of your salary is deducted from your paycheck and applied to your loan)

SUMMARY

In this lesson, you learned your rights and responsibilities as a borrower. You also learned the conditions under which you can defer, reschedule, or cancel federal loans.

20

PAYING BACK
YOUR LOANS

*In this lesson, you will learn how to plan a budget that will allow
you to pay back your loans.*

HOW MUCH SHOULD YOU BORROW?

While most students draw on a variety of resources to finance
their schooling (including savings, investments, and earnings),
a large percentage of students borrow money. Chances are
your financial aid package includes loans. You must carefully
decide how much you can afford to borrow.

> **Borrow as Little as Possible** Follow the advice
> of financial professionals and borrow as little as
> you need to. For when you get out of school, you
> will have to pay back what you owe.

Remember, never borrow before you have to, or borrow more
than you need. Your financial decisions will be based on a
combination of factors, including your:

- Financial award package(s)
- Financial need

- Present and future ability to assume debt

- Projected future earnings

- Level of graduate work (master's or doctoral) and funding availability for your course of study

- Ability to seek out and find outright funding awards (which do not have to be repaid)

ESTIMATING YOUR FUTURE BUDGET

In today's workplace, getting a job is not a sure thing. You can't be certain that your graduate degree will actually land you a job with the salary you expect.

That said, unless you're currently employed and going to school part-time, estimating your future salary will be very difficult. You can get a rough estimate of salaries in your chosen field by reading trade publications (which often conduct salary surveys) and the *Occupational Outlook Handbook*, published by the Bureau of Labor Statistics. Table 20.1 will also give you an idea of the salaries for advanced degree holders in various fields.

TABLE 20.1 COMPARATIVE STARTING SALARIES FOR HOLDERS OF ADVANCED DEGREES

CAREER DESCRIPTION	MASTER'S	PH.D.
Agriculture/Natural Sciences	$28,000–$40,000	$35,000–$50,000
Anthropology	$28,000	$35,000
Chemistry	$31,500	$48,000
Computer Science	$37,500	$40,000–$60,000
Criminal Justice	$24,000–$28,000	no data provided

CAREER DESCRIPTION	MASTER'S	PH.D.
Economics	$32,000	$45,000
Engineering	$35,000	$51,000
Geography	$30,000–$40,000	$35,000–$40,000
Geology	$28,000	$33,500
Journalism	$25,000	no data provided
Mathematics	$30,000	$34,750
Operations Research Analyst	$30,000–$35,000	no data provided
Physical Therapy	$35,000	no data provided
Public Relations Specialist	$27,800	no data provided
Social Work	$25,000	no data provided
Sociology	$27,000	$34,000

Source: *U.S. Department of Labor, Department of Labor Statistics*, Occupational Outlook Handbook, *1995, and* U.S. News & World Report, *"America's Best Graduate Schools," 1995.*

How much of your income should go toward loan repayment? There isn't one answer. The College Board suggests that the total payment for your personal loans (excluding mortgage payments) should not exceed eight percent of your gross monthly income.

Gross income   The money you make before taxes are deducted from your salary.

To get a more realistic look at what you will have to repay out-of-pocket, you should know what your actual take-home pay will be. Table 20.2 shows what salaries of $25,000 and $35,000 yield after taxes are deducted. (Note that Table 20.2 does not include deductions for benefits, such as medical and/or dental plans, or pension plans.) Table 20.2 uses Maryland tax rates for unmarried head-of-household wage-earners claiming one exemption.

TABLE 20.2   MONTHLY PRE- AND AFTER-TAX WAGES

	ANNUAL YEARLY INCOME	
	$25,000.00	**$35,000.00**
Monthly Pretax Wage	$2,083.33	$2,916.66
FICA (Social Security) Tax	$159.37	$223.12
Federal Withholding	$251.00	$453.00
State Withholding	$128.47	$191.47
Actual Take-Home Pay	$1,544.49	$2,049.07

Source: Based on data from the College and University Personnel Association.

ESTIMATING LOAN PAYMENTS

The amount of your loan payments will be based on the interest charged on the loan(s) as well as on the length of the repayment schedule.

Table 20.3 shows the monthly repayments that would accrue for either a subsidized Stafford Loan or an unsubsidized

Stafford Loan for which the student made monthly interest
payments while in school (the interest has not capitalized).

 Use Higher Estimates The government suggests using a 7 percent interest rate when you
estimate your repayment. However, because the
interest rate is variable, and is currently capped
(held) at 8.25 percent, you might consider using
the higher rate in your calculations.

**TABLE 20.3   STANDARD MONTHLY LOAN REPAYMENTS
(10-YEAR TERM)**

LOAN AMOUNT	MONTHLY REPAYMENTS	
	7.0 PERCENT INTEREST RATE	8.25 PERCENT INTEREST RATE
$8,500	$98.69	$104.25
$10,000	$116.11	$122.66
$15,000	$174.17	$183.98
$20,000	$232.22	$245.31
$25,000	$290.28	$306.64
$30,000	$348.33	$367.96
$35,000	$406.38	$429.29
$40,000	$464.44	$490.62

CAN YOU AFFORD A LOAN?

Now that you have an estimated take-home wage, and an idea
of how much your loan repayments will be, ask yourself
whether you can afford to make monthly loan repayments on
top of ordinary living expenses.

Use Table 20.4 to help total the cost of the loan(s) you are
considering.

TABLE 20.4   LOAN MANAGEMENT WORKSHEET

LOAN	LOAN AMOUNT BORROWED	INTEREST RATE	TOTAL MONTHLY PAYMENT	TOTAL INTEREST REPAID
Subsidized Stafford				
Unsubsidized Stafford				
Perkins				
Other				
Other				
Total				

CONSOLIDATING LOANS

Two federal consolidation loans—the Federal Direct Student
Loan (Direct Loan) and the Federal Family Education Loan
(FFEL)—were designed to help borrowers struggling under the
weight of high monthly student loan payments.

Loan Consolidation   A loan consolidation is exactly that—it consolidates your existing loans into one new loan with one lender, who pays off the old loans.

Under a loan consolidation, your monthly payments will be lower, and you may have more time to pay the loan off. However, you will be paying more in interest over the extended repayment period.

Using Loan Consolidation   Although financial professionals usually recommend paying off loans as quickly as possible, your combined debt from undergraduate and graduate school may make loan consolidation a reasonable option. Married couples may be especially interested in this option because It allows them to consolidate their separate student loans into one joint loan.

DIRECT LOAN CONSOLIDATION

On direct loans, the interest rate is variable but is capped at 8.25 percent. Call the Direct Loan Programs Consolidation Department at (800) 848-0982 to see if you qualify for direct loan consolidation. Generally, you must have at least one direct loan to qualify. However, you may also qualify if you are dissatisfied with certain consolidation options offered by private lenders.

FFEL CONSOLIDATION

Under FFEL consolidation, you may pay slightly more interest than you would for separate loans, but you will be paying a fixed interest rate. With FFEL loans, the rate will be the weighted average interest rate of the loans being consolidated and rounded up to the nearest whole percent.

A good source of information about FFEL consolidation loans is the Student Loan Marketing Association (Sallie Mae). For information, write or call:

> Sallie Mae
> Smart Loan Consolidation Center
> P.O. Box 1304
> Merrifield, VA 22116-1304
> (800) 524-9100

Under both direct and FFEL consolidation loans, you will be given different options, including loans with interest-only repayments (in which you pay only the interest on the loan, not the principal) for a short time period.

Table 20.5 represents initial two-year interest-only payments on an FFEL Loan at 9 percent. After two years, the monthly repayments will go up; the actual terms depend on the loan option selected.

TABLE 20.5   TWO-YEAR INTEREST-ONLY REPAYMENT SCHEDULE

AMOUNT OF LOAN	$9,000	$17,000	$30,000	$50,000	$70,000
Typical Repayments	$109	$215	$363	$605	$845
Consolidated Initial Payments	$68	$128	$225	$375	$525

Loan Strategies   Your best loan management strategy is to repay all loans as quickly as possible. You should try to set aside extra money each month and repay more than the required amount. Federal student loans have no prepayment penalty.

SUMMARY

In this lesson, you learned how to estimate your future earnings and determine how much you can afford to take out in loans. You also learned about loan consolidation programs.

STATE STUDENT FINANCIAL AID OFFICES

Following are current addresses and phone numbers for each state's student financial aid office. (Puerto Rico and the Virgin Islands are also included.) Call the agency to find out about state financial aid programs, requirements for resident and non-resident students, and to obtain all application forms, deadline information, and the phone number of your state's Guaranty Agency (the entity responsible for student loans). Information on your state's Guaranty Agency can also be obtained from the Federal Student Aid Information Center at (800) 433-3243.

STATE STUDENT FINANCIAL AID OFFICES

Alabama
Commission on Higher Education
3465 Norman Bridge Road
Montgomery, AL 36104
(334) 281-1921

Alaska
Commission on Postsecondary
  Education
3030 Vintage Boulevard
Juneau, AK 99801
(907) 465-2962

Arizona
Commission for Postsecondary
  Education
2020 North Central Avenue
Phoenix, AZ 85004
(602) 229-2590

Arkansas
Department of Higher Education
114 East Capitol Street
Little Rock, AR 72201
(501) 324-9300

California
Student Aid Commission
P.O. Box 510845
Sacramento, CA 94245
(916) 445-0880

Colorado
Commission on Higher Education
1300 Broadway
Denver, CO 80203
(303) 866-2723

Connecticut
Department of Education
61 Woodland Street
Hartford, CT 06105
(203) 566 3910

Delaware
Commission on Higher Education
820 North French Street
Wilmington, DE 19801
(302) 577-3240

District of Columbia
Office of Postsecondary Education
2100 Martin Luther King, Jr. Avenue
Washington, D.C. 20020
(202) 727-3688

Florida
Office of Student Financial Assistance
1344 Florida Education Center
Tallahassee, FL 32399
(904) 487-0049

Georgia
Student Finance Authority
2082 East Exchange Place
Tucker, GA 30084
(404) 414-3082

Hawaii
Postsecondary Education
Commission
University of Hawaii
2444 Dole Street
Honolulu, HI 96822
(808) 956-8213

Idaho
State Board of Education
P.O. Box 83720
Boise, ID 83720
(208) 334-2270

Illinois
Student Assistance
Commission
1755 Lake Cook Road
Deerfield, IL 60015
(708) 948-8500

Indiana
State Student Assistance
150 West Market Street
Indianapolis, IN 46204
(317) 232-2350

Iowa
College Student Aid
Commission
201 Jewett Building
914 Grand Avenue
Des Moines, IA 50309
(800) 383-4222

Kansas
Board of Regents
700 SW Harrison
Topeka, KS 66603
(913) 296-3421

Kentucky
Higher Education
  Assistance Authority
1050 U.S. 127 South
Frankfort, KY 40601
(800) 928-8926

Louisiana
Office of Higher Education
  Assistance Authority
P.O. Box 91202
Baton Rouge, LA 70821
(800) 259-5626

Maine
Department of Finance Authority
P.O. Box 949
Augusta, ME 04333
(207) 287-2183

Maryland
State Scholarship Administration
16 Francis Street
Annapolis, MD 21401
(410) 974-5370

Massachusetts
Board of Regents
330 Stuart Street
Boston, MA 02116
(617) 727-9420

Michigan
Student Financial Assistance
  Services
P.O. Box 30462
Lansing, MI 48909
(517) 373-3394

Minnesota
Higher Education
  Coordinating Board
550 Cedar Street
St. Paul, MN 55101
(612) 296-3974

Mississippi
Postsecondary Education
  Financial Assistance Board
3825 Ridgewood Road
Jackson, MS 39211
(601) 982-6663

Missouri
Coordinating Board for
  Higher Education
3515 Amazonas Drive
Jefferson City, MO 65109
(314) 751-2361

Montana
State University System
2500 Broadway
Helena, MT 59620
(406) 444-6570

Nebraska
Coordinating Commission
  for Postsecondary Education
P.O. Box 95005
Lincoln, NE 68509
(402) 471-2847

Nevada
Department of Education
400 West King Street
Carson City, NV 89710
(402) 687-3100

New Hampshire
Postsecondary Education
   Commission
Two Industrial Park Drive
Concord, NH 03301
(603) 271-2555

New Jersey
Department of Higher Education
Four Quakerbridge Plaza CN 540
Trenton, NJ 08625
(609) 588-3268

New Mexico
Commission on Higher Education
3900 Osuna NE
Albuquerque, NM 87109
(505) 827-7383

New York
Higher Education Services
   Corporation
99 Washington Avenue
Albany, NY 12255
(518) 474-5642

North Carolina
Education Assistance Authority
P.O. Box 2688
Chapel Hill, NC 27515
(919) 549-8614

North Dakota
Student Financial Assistance
   Program
600 East Boulevard
Bismarck, ND 58505
(701) 224-4114

Ohio
Student Aid Commission
309 South Fourth Street
Columbus, OH 43215
(614) 466-9488

Oklahoma
State Regents for Higher
   Education
500 Education Boulevard
Oklahoma City, OK 73105
(405) 524-9100

Oregon
State Scholarship
   Commission
1500 Valley River Drive
Eugene, OR 97401
(503) 687-7395

Pennsylvania
Higher Education Assistance
   Authority
1200 North Seventh Street
Harrisburg, PA 17102
(717) 257-2800

Puerto Rico
Council on Higher Education
Box 23305 UPR Station
Rio Piedras, PR 00931
(809) 758-3350

Rhode Island
Higher Education Assistance
   Authority
560 Jefferson Boulevard
Warwick, RI 02886
(800) 922-9855

South Carolina
Tuition Grants Commission
1310 Lady Street
Columbia, CS 29211
(803) 734-1200

South Dakota
Department of Education
700 Governors Drive
Pierre, SD 57501
(605) 773-3134

Tennessee
Student Assistance Corporation
404 James Robertson Parkway
Nashville, TN 37243
(615) 741-1346

Texas
Texas College and University
  System Coordinating Board
P.O. Box 12788
Austin, TX 78711
(512) 483-6331

Utah
State Board of Regents
355 West North Temple
Salt Lake City, UT 84180
(801) 321-7205

Vermont
Student Assistance
  Corporation
P.O. Box 2000
Winooski, VT 05404
(800) 642-3177

Virginia
State Council of Higher Education
101 North 14th Street
Richmond, VA 23219
(804) 225-2141

Virgin Islands
Board of Education
P.O. Box 11900
St. Thomas, VI 00801
(809) 774-4546

Washington
Higher Education Coordinating
  Board
917 Lakeridge Way
Olympia, WA 98504
(206) 753-7850

West Virginia
State College and University
  Systems Central Office
P.O. Box 4007
Charleston, WV 25364
(304) 347-1211

Wisconsin
Higher Education Aids Board
131 West Wilson Street
Madison, WI 53707
(608) 267-2206

Wyoming
Wyoming Community College
  Commission
122 West 25th Street
Cheyenne, WY 82002
(307) 777-7763

Source: Federal Student Financial Aid Handbook, *1995-1996.*

FINANCIAL AID
GLOSSARY

Assistantships   Financial aid provided for performing work (usually on a part-time basis). Types of assistantships include teaching, research, administrative, and residence. Assistantships are usually awarded according to merit.

Campus-Based Programs   Federal aid programs administered by a school's financial aid administrator. For graduate study, these programs include Federal Work-Study (FWS) and Perkins Loans.

Consolidation Loan Program   Federal loan consolidation program enabling students to combine different types of federal loans to simplify repayment after graduation. The lender pays off the existing loans; the borrower then repays the consolidation loan. Borrowers have from 10 to 30 years to repay it.

Cooperative Education   Work-study arrangement in which the student receives academic credit for work outside the school. Students work full- or part-time as salaried employees for participating companies.

Cost of Attendance (COA)   Also called Student Budget. The total amount it will cost a student to go to school, usually expressed as a yearly figure. The COA covers tuition and fees; housing; food; and allowances for books, supplies, transportation, loan fees, dependent care, costs related to a disability, and miscellaneous expenses. For part-time students, the COA does not include room and board.

Default   Borrower's failure to repay a loan according to the terms agreed to. Default may also result from failure to submit requests for deferment or cancellation on time. Borrowers in default may be subject to garnishment of wages, credit difficulties, and other penalties.

Endowments   As pertaining to financial aid, that portion of private donations to schools which is administered by the financial aid office in the form of loans, grants, scholarships, and other awards.

Expected Family Contribution (EFC)   For graduate students, this is the amount you and your spouse are expected to contribute to your educational costs. This figure is subtracted from the Cost of Attendance to determine your financial need. Factors such as taxable and nontaxable income, assets (such as savings and checking accounts), and benefits (such as unemployment or social security) are all considered in this calculation. If you're married, your spouse's contribution is also calculated. No student contribution is calculated for eligibility for unsubsidized Stafford Loans.

Federal Work-Study (FWS)   Federal subsidy program that provides jobs for students with financial need, allowing them to earn money to pay educational expenses. The program encourages community service work and work related to the student's course of study.

Fellowship   An outright stipend usually awarded on a merit basis.

Financial Aid   Financial assistance from government, institutional, and private sources given to supplement the student's family contribution.

Financial Aid Package   The total amount of financial aid a student receives. Federal and nonfederal aid, such as scholarships, loans, or work-study, are combined to help the student.

One of the major responsibilities of a school's financial aid administrator is to use available resources to give each student the best possible package.

Financial Aid PROFILE   Form from the College Scholarship Service (CSS). This form has replaced the CSS Financial Aid Form. Many schools use this need-analysis form along with the Free Application for Federal Student Aid.

Forbearance   Regarding the repayment of loans, forbearance means the lender has agreed to let the borrower defer payments for a period of time. During this period of time, interest accrues on the loan. The act of forbearance is solely at the discretion of the lender.

Free Application for Federal Student Aid (FAFSA)
Needs analysis form required for obtaining all federal aid as well as much state aid. Many schools use it as their only financial aid application form.

Grant   Outright award usually awarded to students in par ticular fields of study.

Institution   A postsecondary educational institution. The terms "institution" and "school" are used interchangeably in this book.

Internship   Work-study arrangement allowing students to gain practical experience through off-campus work with participating companies. In some instances, stipends are paid to the student by the outside organization.

Merit-Based Aid   Outright awards, such as fellowships, grants, and scholarships, that may or may not have a work-related component. Much merit-based aid is determined by GRE scores.

Need Analysis   Process of analyzing the financial information on the student's financial aid application and calculating the amount the family (student) can contribute to his or her educational costs.

Need-Based Aid   Aid awarded on the basis of financial need usually determined by the government need formula: Cost of Attendance (COA) minus Expected Family Contribution equals Student's Financial Need.

Origination Fee   Loan process fee charged to borrower by lender, usually calculated as a percentage of the loan amount. On federal loans, this fee is deducted from the loan amount before the borrower receives the loan.

Outright Award   Financial aid that does not have to be repaid. Loans are not outright awards.

Perkins Loan   Federal low-interest loan to students with exceptional financial need. Federal Perkins Loans are administered through a school's financial aid office; the school is the lender and the loan is made with government funds. Borrowers must repay this loan.

Professional Judgment   Authority of the financial aid administrator to make individual adjustments in determining financial need. For graduate students, the administrator is allowed to adjust the components of the student's Cost of Attendance (budget) and adjust the data elements used to calculate the Expected Family Contribution (EFC). These adjustments must be made on a case-by-case basis, and the adjustment reasons must be documented in the student's file.

Promissory Note   The binding legal document a borrower signs to get a student loan. It lists borrowing terms and repayment terms. It includes information about the loan's interest rate and about deferment and cancellation provisions.

State Guaranty Agency   The state agency responsible for administering student loans. Telephone numbers of state agencies can be found by calling the Federal Student Aid Information Center at 800-433-3243.

Statement of Educational Purpose/Certification Statement on Refunds and Default   Statement that must be signed by the borrower to receive federal student aid. It signifies that the borrower does not owe a refund on a federal grant, is not in default on a federal loan, and that the amount borrowed doesn't exceed the allowable limits. Borrowers also agree to use their student aid only for education-related purposes.

Student Aid Report (SAR)   Document received from the FAFSA processor about four weeks after submitting the original FAFSA form. The SAR must be carefully read and verified to ensure accuracy of all data.

Subsidized Stafford Loan (formerly Guaranteed Student Loan—GSL)   Federally subsidized low-interest loans available to students who demonstrate financial need. The federal government pays interest on the loan until the borrower begins repayment and during authorized periods of loan deferment. Students do not begin repayment until after graduation.

Targeted Aid   Both outright awards and loans from government, institutional, and private sources earmarked for specific groups of students. These special aid programs often aid minorities and women.

Unmet Need   Portion of the financial aid package which the student is eligible to receive but which the school is unable to fund.

Unsubsidized Stafford Loan Federal loan not awarded on the basis of need. Interest is charged on the loan from the time the loan is disbursed until it's paid in full. Payment of interest and principal can be deferred while student is in school.

Verification Procedure used by the school financial aid office for verifying the accuracy of the financial aid data filled out on the FAFSA and other financial aid applications. Students may be asked to fill out additional forms or submit additional documentation, such as tax returns and earnings statements. Some schools verify 100 percent of all financial aid applications; others do not.

INDEX

A-B

academic quality of schools
and programs, 10-12
AchieverLoans, 41
admission deadlines, 106, 108
advantages of deferring grad
school, 4-6
assistantships, 27, 50-51, 141
attendance costs vs. financial
aid, 18-19
awards, outright, 144
   deadlines, 109
   financial aid eligibility, 61
   merit-based aid, 143
   resources, 55
      award programs, 59-60
      bookstores, 59
      computer online
       information, 56-57
      The Foundation
       Center, 58
      libraries, 56
      scholarship search
       firms, 58
      schools, 55-56
   taxes, 61
   types, 54-55

benefits of graduate degree,
1-2

C

calendars, deadline, preparing,
106-107
canceling loans, 124-125
capitalizing loans, 37
certificates of deposit (CDs), 88
choosing schools, 10
COA, *see* costs of attendance
computers, software, Student
Loan Counselor, 16-17
consolidation loan
programs, 141
cooperative education
programs, 52, 141
costs
   attendance costs vs.
      financial aid, 18-19
   of attendance (COA), 141
   financial planning, 16-17
   personal expenses, 19-21
   total costs, 21-22
   tuition, 17-19
credit unions, 43

D-E

deadlines
   admission, 106, 108
   deadline calendars,
      preparing, 106-107
   financial aid, 106, 108-110
   testing, 105-108
defaulting on loans, 120,
   125-126, 141

deferring loans, 122
direct loans, *see* Federal Direct
  Student Loan Program
disabled students, financial
  aid, special funding
  opportunities, 79
doctoral vs. master's degrees,
  9-10

employee tuition assistance
  programs, 42-43
endowments, financial aid,
  142
expected family contribution
  (EFC), 101, 142
expenses, *see* costs

F

faculty interviews, 12
FAFSA, *see* Free Application
  for Federal Student Aid
Federal Direct Student Loan
  Program, 34, 133
Federal Family Education Loan
  (FFEL) Program, 34, 134-135
federal grants, *see* grants
federal loans, *see* loans
Federal Methodology (FM)
  formula, financial aid need,
  24
Federal Student Aid
  Information Center, 25, 136
Federal Work-Study (FWS)
  program, 48-49, 142
fellowships, 26, 51-52, 142
  resources, 62-63
    award programs, 66-67
    computer online resources,
      64-65
    libraries, 65-66
  see also outright awards
FFEL, *see* Federal Family Education Loan (FFEL) Program
fields of study, resources, 2-3

financial aid, 142
  applying for
    departmental assistance,
      93
    forms, 93-94
    Free Application for
      Federal Student Aid
      (FAFSA) forms, 97-100
    obtaining applications,
      92
    process, 91-92
    PROFILE, 104, 143
    requesting information
      from financial aid
      offices, 94-96
    researching sources, 93
    special circumstances,
      103-104
    Student Aid Reports
      (SAR), 100-103, 145
  assistantships, 141
  award packages
    accepting, 117-118
    award letters, 112-113
    choosing best package,
      114-116
    cost factors, 116-117
    loans, 116
    negotiating, 117
    receiving, 111-112
  campus-based programs,
    141
  deadlines, 106, 108-110
  endowments, 142
  Federal Student Aid
    Information Center, 136
  merit-based, 25
  need analysis, 144
  need-based, 24-25, 144
  options, 45-46
  packages, 142
  percentage of students
    receiving, 27-30
  professional judgment, 144
  sources, 23

special funding
opportunities
international students,
79-80
overseas study, 78-79
resources, 74-75
students with
disabilities, 79
veterans, 78
women, 75-77
state student financial aid
offices, 136-140
stipends, 50
targeted aid, 25, 145
types, 26-27
unmet need, 145
verification procedure, 146
see also grants; loans;
outright awards; work
programs
financial standing, *see* net
worth, calculating
forbearance, loans, 122-123,
143
foreign students, financial aid,
special funding opportunities, 79-80
401(k) retirement savings
program, loans, 43
Free Application for Federal
Student Aid (FAFSA) form,
31, 97-100, 143
full-time vs. part-time, 7
academic quality of school
and program, 10-12
choosing schools, 10
costs of schools, 12
housing, 14-15
location and safety of
schools, 13-14
master's vs. doctoral
degrees, 9-10
size of schools, 13
FWS, *see* Federal Work-Study
(FWS) program

G

GradEXCEL/GradSHARE, 41
Graduate Record
Examinations (GRE) testing
deadlines, 107
grants, 26, 51-52, 143
applying for
procedures, 68-70
proposal structure, 71-72
resources, 72-73
strategies, 70
writing style /
organization, 71
federal, resources, 62-63
award programs, 66-67
computer online
resources, 64-65
libraries, 65-66
state, matching grant
programs, 46-47
GRE, *see* Graduate Record
Examinations (GRE) testing
deadlines
gross income, 129
Guaranteed Student Loan
(GSL), *see* loans, Stafford
guaranty agencies, loans, 136,
145

H-K

home equity loans, 40
housing, 14-15

income, gross, 129
institutions, 143
international students,
financial aid, special funding
opportunities, 79-80
internships, 52-53, 143
interviews, faculty, 12

L

loans
  401(k) retirement savings
    programs, 43
  canceling 124-125
  capitalizing, 37
  consolidating, 132-135, 141
  counseling, 119-120
  credit unions, 43
  defaulting on, 120, 125-126,
    141
  deferring, 122
  federal, 32-38, 145, 146
  forbearance, 122-123, 143
  forgiveness (cancellation)
    programs, 46
  guaranty agencies, 136
  home equity, 40
  origination fees, 144
  Perkins, 32-33, 124-125
  private
    employee assistance
      programs, 42-44
    lenders, 34
    private programs, 41
    researching, 39-40
    school programs, 42
  promissory notes, 144
  repayment
    borrowing amounts,
      127-128
    estimating future budgets,
      128-130
    estimating loan pay-
      ments, 130-131
    responsibilities and rights,
      119-122
    total costs, 132
  Stafford, 33-38, 125, 145-
    146
  state, 46
  TERI Alternative Loan
    Programs and Professional
    Education Plans (PEP), 41
location of schools, 13-14

M

master's vs. doctoral
  degrees, 9-10
MAT, *see* Miller Analogies Test
merit-based financial aid,
  25, 143
military service, benefits, 5
Miller Analogies Test (MAT),
  107
minorities, financial aid,
  special funding opportunities, 75-77
money-market deposit
  accounts (MMDAs), 87
mutual funds, 87-88

N

National Center for
  Cooperative Education, 52
need analysis,
  financial aid, 144
need-based financial aid,
  24-25, 144
Nellie Mae, 41
net worth, calculating
  amount of need,
    estimating, 85
  assets, 81-82
  liabilities, 82
  worksheet, 83-85
New England Education Loan
  Marketing Corp.
  (Nellie Mae), 41

O

Option 4 Loan Program, 41
origination fees, loan, 144
outright awards, 144
  deadlines, 109
  financial aid eligibility, 61
  merit-based aid, 143
  resources, 55
    award programs, 59-60
    bookstores, 59

computer online
information, 56-57
The Foundation Center,
58
libraries, 56
scholarship search
firms, 58
schools, 55-56
taxes, 61
types, 54-55
overseas study, financial aid,
special funding
opportunities, 78-79

P-R

passbook savings accounts, 87
percentage of students
receiving financial aid, 27-30
personal expenses, 19-21
private loans
lenders, 34
researching, 39-40
employee assistance
programs, 42-44
private programs, 41
school programs, 42
private vs. public schools,
tuition, 17-19
professional judgment, 144
PROFILE, 104
PROFILE financial aid
forms, 143
programs, academic
quality, 10-12
promissory notes, loans, 144
public ivys, 47

S

safety of schools, 13-14
salaries, starting, for advanced
degree holders, 128-129
Sallie Mae, see Student Loan
Marketing Association
savings plans

certificates of deposit
CDs), 88
estimating needs, 86-87
money-market deposit
accounts (MMDAs), 87
mutual funds, 87-88
passbook savings
accounts, 87
resources, 88-89
savings bonds, 88
special college savings
plans, 89
treasury bills/notes, 88
scholarships, 26
resources, 62-63
award programs, 66-67
computer online resources,
64-66
see also outright awards
schools
academic quality, 10-12
choosing, 10
costs, 12, 141
attendance costs vs.
financial aid, 18-19
financial planning, 16-17
housing, 14-15
personal expenses, 19-21
total costs, 21-22
tuition, 17-19
resources, 55-56
location/safety, 13-14
size, 13
student budgets, 141
state grants, grant matching
programs, 46-47
state guaranty agencies, 145
state loans, 46
state student financial aid
offices, 136-140
Statement of Educational
Purpose/Certification
Statement on Refunds and
Default, 145
stipends, 50

Student Aid Reports (SAR),
100-103, 145
student budgets, 141
Student Loan Counselor
financial software, 16-17
Student Loan Marketing
Association (Sallie Mae), 134
subsidized Stafford loans,
35-36, 145

T

targeted financial aid, 25, 145
taxes
financial aid deadlines, 110
outright awards, 61
TERI Alternative Loan Programs and Professional
Education Plans (PEP), 41
Test of English as a Foreign
Language (TOEFL), 107
testing deadlines, 105-108
total costs of attendance, 21-22
treasury bills/notes, 88
tuition, 17-19

U-Z

U.S. Department of
Education, 32
unmet need, financial aid, 145
unsubsidized Stafford loans,
36-38, 146

verification procedures, 146
veterans, financial aid, special
funding opportunities, 78

when to go to school, 4-6
women, financial aid, special
funding opportunities, 75-77
work programs
assistantships, 50-51, 141
cooperative education
programs, 52, 141
federal work-study (FWS),
26, 43-44, 48-49, 142

fellowships, 51-52, 142
grants, 51-52
internships, 52-53, 143
working vs. going to
graduate school, 3-6